Contents

Barracuda Alert. 1

Your Attorney General Wants You 8

This Agency Has Sharp Teeth 23

Barracudas You Used To Know (and Swim With). 34

The Right Role in the Melodrama 45

The Department of Defense Plays Offense 61

Not a Class Act. 70

I Don't Like You Anymore 83

Caveat Vendor 96

When It's Hot, It's Hot 108

Florida 2000 116

The Moral of the Story 130

Endnotes 140

I would like to express special thanks to a bright and capable young lawyer, Christopher Schweickert, for his invaluable assistance in helping research and compile illustrations for this book. I am also grateful to my assistant, Debbie Hobson, for her efforts, which were flawless as usual, and, of course, my colleagues at Dorsey & Whitney LLP, who through heroic interventions have on more than one occasion pulled me back from the precipice of disaster.

To Don,

the world's best hockey
coach — from the former
next door neighbor
of Herb Brooks - - -

Best wishes,

11/27/07

Barracuda Bait

by

Roger Magnuson

Landsen-Holm Publishers

Copyright © 2007. Roger J. Magnuson

ISBN: 978-0-9798498-0-0
Library of Congress Control Number: 2007933216

Printed in the United States of America

Chapter 1

Barracuda Alert

It was a brilliant May day in a small harbor off the shores of the island of St. John. The sun dappled waters off the side of the sailboat looked inviting. The amateur snorkeler in me reacted like Odysseus of old when hearing the seductive invitations of the Sirens in the waves. I jumped over the side of the boat thinking to inspect Neptune's Chambers.

The coral was lovely. The multicolored fish swam by lazily, in schools and with a certain esprit decor. Life was good. As I turned back to examine the coral reef from a new angle, however, I came face to face with an unexpected visitor. Though piscatorially challenged, I appeared to be face-to-face with a barracuda. Put another way, a barracuda appeared to be face-to-face with me. It was clear that I was looking at him. It was also clear that he was looking at me. Feeling rather like Little Red Riding Hood admiring grandma's teeth, I stared at him face to face. The sight was daunting. He had sharper teeth than I had. Memories of Berthold Brecht's Three Penny Opera came to mind. Or, more precisely, Louis Armstrong singing Mac the Knife. Knowing that discretion was the better part of valor, I decided to swim away and hope that he did not feel the liberty to follow me.

I pulled myself back onto the boat, using a rope ladder, and flopped on deck. In talking to the skipper, there was good news. He told me it was fortunate that I had no affinity for gold chains or other titillating ornamentation. If I had been wearing a tasteful nose ring, or diamond earring, or a twenty-four carat gold necklace, I might have stirred up the covetous instincts of my fishy friend who, excited by the prospect of sharing such ornamentation, would likely have wanted a piece of it. And of me. Never did I appreciate more the unintended consequences of good taste. Notwithstanding the good news from my friendly skipper, I decided not to go back in the water. From then on I've preferred waters that were not infested by such aggressive companions.

Not that I have anything against barracudas. They just do what comes naturally. What they do naturally, however, poses some risks to me.

When I got back to St. Thomas that evening and walked through the port in the city of Charlotte Amalie, I had other barracudas to worry about. I had been warned. While most residents of that sunny island are congenial, there do lurk in the crevices of the rocks around the harbor a different kind of barracuda. When they see tourists in loud sport coats, sporting bulges that suggest thick wallets, or wearing attractive jewelry, they also can close fast. They observe, then come closer to examine potential prey. And if the glitter is attractive enough, they strike. It just comes naturally.

> A new **civil** lawsuit is filed every blink of your eye— every 1.93 seconds.
>
> A new **criminal** case is filed every other beat of your heart – every 2.05 seconds. [1.1]

Since it was my last evening in the Caribbean before returning to a cold early March in Minneapolis, I decided to have a leisurely dinner harborside in the city. Afterward, I walked up the narrow streets to the Villa Santa Anna, a villa that purportedly was once owned by General Santa Anna. It was my usual practice to sit out on mild nights under the stars on the good general's veranda, looking at the large cruise ships and sparkling yachts owned by Saudi Arabian sheiks illuminating the harbor below. Since someone was already occupying my favorite chair (there were others, but I am a creature of habit), I decided to retire early. I went into the room. I reflected on the safety and security of the bed. I meditated on the Psalms ("I will lay me down in peace and sleep"). I went to sleep. A few minutes later, when I was already groggy, I heard the door knob jiggle, then a knock. I considered getting up to see what was happening. Figuring it was the turn down service and concluding that even a Godiva chocolate was not worth the disruption of my slumber, I rolled over and hoped the staff would go away.

The next morning I left my room to find that the villa was in a stir. There had been a shocking occurrence during the night. A robber,

> When I'm rich—not before—I can buy a Z4.
>
> —A young lawyer

armed with a revolver, had held up the man who had occupied my chair on the veranda only minutes after I had walked past him. He had then systematically robbed all the other residents of the villa. Indeed, he had robbed people right outside my window. He had held a gun to the head of a woman, six months pregnant, right outside my room door. Determined to rob every occupant in the eight-unit villa, he had been the one who had jiggled my door knob, trying to get in, revolver in hand, to terrorize me. He had ordered the woman to knock on my door. There was no answer. The door remained locked. Distracted or discouraged, he gave up. As it turned out, everyone in the entire villa had been robbed, except me.

The surprising thing, the ultimate irony of the story, was that I was the only person he had intended to rob. Only me. Something about my blazer or appearance or choice of restaurants had excited his larcenous heart. He had stalked me invisibly up the narrow, twisting path to the villa. I had been unaware of his footsteps behind me, or his predatory interest. If I had followed my normal routine, I would have felt his teeth. He was my barracuda. I was his prey. At such moments, one rejoices to have a guardian angel.

The biggest verdict so far in a product liability case that wasn't a class action, $4.9 billion, was handed down in the summer of 1999 in California. A jury held General Motors responsible for non-fatal burns in a two-car wreck caused by a drunken driver who wasn't even sued. The judge cut the award as excessive—to $1.2 billion. [1.2]

But in a very real sense the two barracudas were not far different from each other. My stalker was also doing what came naturally. He patrolled his own harbor. He also was excited by the flash of exciting attractions. He struck as necessary to satisfy his special appetites.

If he had been successful in biting me, I would certainly have had no moral culpability. He was the robber. I should have been his victim. But while I might not have had any moral culpability, my cluelessness about the existence of such predators in those different waters, whether plying their trade in the bay or along the cobblestones of the narrow streets of St. Thomas, was reckless. And potentially expensive, to my wallet and maybe to my health. Neither barracuda, if the truth be told, cared a great deal about my welfare.

There is, of course, a moral here. Corporations and successful business people enjoy the fruits of their own success. They enjoy their snorkeling. They visit their favorite restaurants. They swim in their own sun dappled waters. They have views of illuminated harbors.

But lurking in those waters and hidden in those back alleys are some curious barracudas. And the wise swimmer/stroller needs to pay attention to the kind of ornamentation that attracts them.

Such caution is sensible. It is sensible because barracudas do what comes naturally. They have no compunction about taking a bite out of someone's epidermis. In the environment where they feel comfortable, they have several competitive advantages over the most buff human swimmer. They are sleek. They are swift. They swim better in their natural waters than the best human swimmer. They are sharp toothed. They are more than a little slippery. They bite you. And you have little opportunity to bite back.

The barracudas who swim in corporate waters are similar. It might be the sharp-eyed investigator from the SEC looking carefully to see whether some executive has sold stock shortly before negative news. It may be the sleek, B.M.W.–driving, class-action lawyer attracted by the sudden downturn in the price of a company's shares or an unexpected restatement of earnings. It may be a state attorney general, thinking to himself that he deserves a promotion to Governor of the state, and looking for the scalp of a prominent business executive to show off to a skeptical electorate to demonstrate how tough he is. It may be an ideological litigant, weary of the slow pace of reform in Congress or in the state legislature. He wants to take a piece out of a target industry or a company that he believes is not a good corporate citizen. It might be a U.S. attorney, armed with a staggering arsenal of remedies, tired of putting lower class drug dealers into penitentiaries, eager to find some corporations, ideally some executive, to put behind bars.

A New Orleans lawyer won a $3.4 billion verdict against CSX Transportation and four co-defendants in 1997. The case stemmed from a 1987 train explosion in Louisiana that forced thousands from their homes but caused no deaths or serious injuries. [1.3]

In the old days, corporate citizens had less to worry about. Blackstone had, after all, laid it down in his famous Commentaries. Corporations cannot commit crimes, he wrote, because corporations are fictitious persons. Corporations were typically the aggressors. Big Bank pulled the plug on some hapless customer. The corporate landlord threw out onto the streets some hapless tenant.

But given the changing environment of the past two or three decades, it is increasingly clear that corporations, and not just badly run corporations, have frequently become the victims of attacks by others. Their treasuries, and their reputations, can look like the surfboard that washed up on the shores of Kauai a few years back. It was half gone. It was cut in half, leaving a jagged cut. The human being who

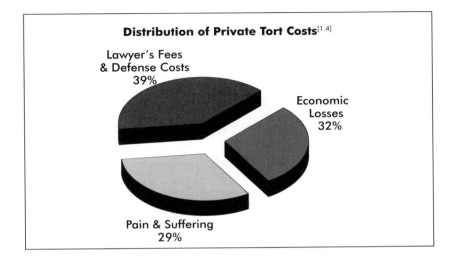

Distribution of Private Tort Costs[1.4]

Lawyer's Fees & Defense Costs 39%

Economic Losses 32%

Pain & Suffering 29%

had been riding on top of it was never found. A surfer had attracted the wrong kind of attention.

The mutilated surfboards of our day are congressional hearings on the bankruptcy of a giant corporation, press conferences announcing indictment of a big company, a huge class-action filed days after the dismal earnings report, a grinning state regulator announcing on the evening news some action against a local bank or real estate company, news of a bet-the-company lawsuit making the front pages of the business section of a local newspaper, a terrifying letter from the SEC.

Such events can make a person nervous. It can make your entire life, with any of its notable achievements, pass before your eyes. It can be, in the words of William Faulkner in his Nobel Prize acceptance speech, "the dingdong of doom dingdonging."

In the face of such risks, many executives become fatalists. Que sera sera, they say, whatever will be will be. Like the tragic hero in a classical drama, like Antigone, they will find the business end of fate biting their backsides. According to some mysterious ordering they cannot predict or protect themselves from.

Fatalism has some foundation. The ball takes funny bounces on an uneven infield. There are many imponderables. Good things happen to bad people and bad things happen to good people. A corporation of any size will experience unexpected turbulence.

But it is also true that it is possible to generalize, to take precautions, to know what attracts the local barracudas. And once knowledgeable

➤ **Hookers v. Hollywood.** A group claiming to represent prostitutes, drug abusers, and panhandlers wrote to several Hollywood film companies in August 2002 seeking cash compensation for depriving them of business opportunities and displacing them from neighborhoods during the filming of various movies. [1.5a]

➤ **In Belton, S.C.,** Olene Burton took the infamous case of the hot McDonald's coffee to a new level by suing Krispy Kreme, claiming a hot doughnut burned her wrist. [1.5]

➤ **Taco Bell was sued** for serving a beef burrito to a Hindu—for whom eating beef is sacrilegious—instead of the chicken burrito he ordered. [1.5]

➤ **Most Valuable Lawsuit.** Proving that litigation madness isn't limited to the U.S. alone, a father in New Brunswick, Canada, is suing an amateur hockey league for $300,000 after his son failed to win the league's Most Valuable Player award. The lawsuit seeks psychological and punitive damages, and it demands that the trophy be taken away from the player to whom it was awarded and given to his son. [1.5b]

➤ **A D.C. lawyer who sued his own mother** settled for $15,000, then threatened to sue a reporter for writing about it. [1.5]

➤ **A divorce lawyer** from Fullerton, Calif., sued GTE for $100,000 after her practice was listed in the Yellow Pages under "reptiles." [1.5]

➤ **The American Civil Liberties Union** sued the Suns baseball team in Hagerstown, MD, for giving church-goers a $2 discount on Easter. [1.5]

➤ **The California** District Court of Appeal reinstated a man's lawsuit against Hertz for charging him $3.19 a gallon to fill the tank of a rental car (at a time when gas was approximately $1.25/gal.). [1.5]

➤ **Monkey Business.** A group of legal activists, including Harvard Law professor Laurence Tribe, is pressing to grant chimpanzees legal standing in court, similar to that of children. If the group has its way, a chimpanzee theoretically could win an injunction against a medical researcher or a roadside zoo. [1.5c] about the barracuda's inclinations, a person can often swim quietly away without losing any skin.

And one need not always be on the defense. The barracudas are, after all, sometimes taken by human beings. There are ways to even the odds.

This book is the product of many confrontations, on behalf of many clients, in the face of many barracudas, in many different jurisdictions around the country, and around the world. It is written from the premise that it is better to bait a barracuda than to be barracuda bait.

It seeks to identify the sharpest toothed of the often unseen swimming companions of the contemporary executive and to show what attracts and repels them. It confirms the worst downside of the barracuda attack, illustrating sad episodes of some bad bites happening to undeserving swimmers. It shows why such attacks happened. But it also shows that losses are not inevitable. And it shows that it is possible to bite back. By creative and aggressive approaches, barracudas can be taught a lesson or two. There are certain kinds of prey prudence indicates should not be attacked.

I took no great joy in the news that all of my neighbors at the Villa Santana had been robbed except me. I commiserated with them. I expressed my sympathy.

But in the final analysis, I was not unhappy that it had not happened to me. After two successful escapes from two different kinds of barracudas in one day, I happily boarded a flight home to Minneapolis the next morning, safe in the security provided by living on a lake that still had three inches of ice separating human beings from sharp-toothed northern pike just below the surface of the water.

Chapter 2

Your Attorney General Wants You

"Regulation is out, litigation is in. The era of big government may be over, but the era of regulation through litigation has just begun."[2.1]

—*Robert Reich*

"If you laid out all of our laws end to end, there would be no end."[2.2]

—*Mark Twain*

They knew it would not be easy. The Milwaukee Braves were a local and by now legendary institution. After years of World Series where the only transportation necessary for fans of the competing teams was on subways between boroughs in New York City, a new city was heard from.

The steely arms and quick wrists of Henry Aaron hammered out home runs. Warren Spahn and Lew Burdette confused batters, Spahn with elegant stuff that would win him 369 career victories and Burdette with copious spit that caused the baseball to reel like a staggering drunk. The meaty Joe Adcock was an intimidating presence at first base, and the agile Johnny Logan could hit and field at shortstop. Billy Bruton chased down fly balls to the remotest corners of center field. Eddie Matthews hit more home runs than any third baseman in history and, with Hank Aaron, formed the most prodigious homerun tandem ever joined on one team. The stolid Del Crandall was a backstop behind the plate. And all of this in a city cold and obscure by New York City sensibilities, with little competition for entertainment. The Braves were the only show in town.

The inhabitants of beer town went crazy in the first World Series year, 1959. Grade school students went back and forth to school with

$130,000 an Hour

"In January 1998, Texas Attorney General Dan Morales (D.) announced that his trial-lawyer team—'junkyard dogs,' he called them—had reached a $17.3-billion settlement with the tobacco industry, which led to a stupendous $3.3-billion fee awarded by federal arbitrators. Houston attorney Marc Murr, a Morales friend and fundraiser, demanded $520 million. The other trial-lawyer firms said Murr had played no visible role in the case. Secretly Murr and Morales selected the three members of a state arbitration panel to weigh the merits of Murr's claim, then appeared before the panel as its only witnesses. The panel awarded Murr $260 million—or $130,000 for every hour he claimed to have worked on the case.

"Last May [1999] a new Texas attorney general, John Cornyn (R.), filed papers in federal court charging that Morales had created bogus contracts for Murr. The trial lawyer's fee award, he said, had been 'procured by fraud.' One day later Murr withdrew his request for the $260 million. The FBI entered the case, and a federal grand jury has convened. Morales has denied any wrongdoing, and Murr claims that he worked behind the scenes as a strategist.

"Meanwhile, trial lawyers are looking for new worlds to conquer...." [2.3]

transistor radios pressed to their ears. The insufferable Yankees and long-suffering Dodgers had to get out of the way to make room for the new powerhouse. They were the Milwaukee Braves. Two years, two World Series. The new kid on the block. They were full of future Hall-of-Famers and excited the imagination of the nation.

But Milwaukee was a small market. In later years, attendance declined as the team declined. The stars got old. The honeymoon was over. County Stadium became empty, old and dismal.

It was time to move the franchise. Atlanta, Georgia, the center of the new south, began to flirt. The flirtation became more serious. A new and larger market, a new and larger stadium. In the end, the temptations proved too much for local family ownership.

The Braves announced they were going to move.

The owners expected controversy. No area likes to lose a professional sports franchise. But America was a free country. People can do what they want with their own possessions. The local populace would just have to understand.

But the attorney general of the state had other ideas. This controversy to him was like iron to Bismarck. It was an invitation to legal warfare. He decided to strike.

His strike was successful. He convinced a Milwaukee state court to enjoin the move to Atlanta. He convinced the court to order a draft of major league baseball players to supplement the team's weaknesses at various positions. He would rewrite the rules of professional baseball using the local courts.

The result was a curious three-ring circus. The attorney general of Georgia, upon hearing of the Wisconsin intervention, was not amused. He struck back. Going before the local Georgia court, he convinced the local judge to grant a mandatory injunction, compelling the Braves to move to Atlanta. Now the owners of the Braves had to deal with two orders, ordering them to do contradictory things. They were required to move, and they were required not to move.

Soon another jurisdiction weighed in. A Texas court, this time a federal court, decided that the Wisconsin court was wrong, and undeterred by 1500 miles of distance or federal court-state court comity, it felt empowered to correct the error. It sought to order the court to rescind its injunction.

As any child can attest, it is difficult to watch three entertaining rings at the same time under the big top. One might think that such fraternal competition among competing jurisdictions is one reason why the Constitution of the United States has the Commerce Clause. But no matter, the controversy continued nonetheless.

The award for a profile in courage goes to the Supreme Court of the state of Wisconsin. It ultimately decided to reverse the County Court and let the Braves move. Legal principle conquered pragmatic politics. The Braves moved and the rest, as they say, is history.

Later in the face of potential contraction of a neighboring franchise, the Minnesota Twins, announced by the one-time owner of a new Milwaukee franchise and now commissioner of baseball, Bud Selig, the lower courts were equally parochial but the Supreme Court of Minnesota was not so courageous. The Twins were compelled not to go out of business and play one more year in their Metrodome. The message of both cases is clear. The barracudas in state regulatory offices swim swiftly into politically charged controversies, finding them as attractive as the barracuda finds the glitter of gold. Given the right target, they will strike. They will protect local interests, no matter how parochial. They will get their pictures in the local papers when they attack the rich and successful. They will be more mindful of the polls than the precedents.

And there is an additional moral to the story. Every one of the justices of the Wisconsin Supreme Court who supported the right of the

The Victory Cigar[2.4]
Selected Tobacco Fees Awarded to Trial Lawyers, Inc. (as of Dec. 2002)

State	Payments to State	Awards to Lawyers	Law Firms
Mississippi	$4.1 billion	$1.4 billion	Richard Scruggs, Ness Motley
Florida	$13.2 billion	$3.4 billion	Scruggs, Ness Motley, nine Florida firms
Texas	$17.365 billion	$3.299 billion	Scruggs, Ness Motley, five Texas firms
Massachusetts	$8.3 billion	$775 million*	Ness Motley, Lieff Cabraser, four Boston firms
Hawaii	$1.38 billion	$90 million*	Ness Motley, Scruggs, four Hawaii firms
Illinois	$9.3 billion	$121 million*	Hagens German, Lieff Cabraser, two other firms
Iowa	$1.9 billion	$85 million	Ness Motley, six other firms
Louisiana	$4.6 billion	$575 million*	Seventeen firms
Kansas	$1.767 billion	$54 million*	Ness Motley, Scruggs, two Kansas firms
Ohio	$10.1 billion	$265 million	Ness Motley, Scruggs, five other firms
Oklahoma	$2 billion	$250 million	Ness Motley, Scruggs, four Oklahoma firms
Puerto Rico	$2.2 billion	$75 million*	Ness Motley, Scruggs, two local firms
New Mexico	$1.25 billion	$24.5 million*	Two local firms
South Carolina	$2.3 billion	$82.5 million*	Ness Motley
Utah	$1 billion	$64.85 million*	Glauque Crockett Bendinger & Peterson, Ness Motley
California	$25 billion	$637.5 million*	Milberg Weiss, Lieff Cabraser, two California firms
Michigan	$8.7 billion	$450 million*	Ness Motley, Scruggs
New York	$25 billion	$625 million*	Ness Motley, Scruggs, Hagens Berman, three local firms

*In litigation. States have sued to reduce lawyer' fees.
Source: The American Lawyer, December 2002

owners to move the franchise was voted out of office at the next judicial election.

Most state attorneys general are, of course, fine people. They are generally a responsible lot. But then again most fish are not barracudas. It is the barracuda, however, that has the teeth.

In North Dakota some years ago, a commissioner of insurance decided to step down unexpectedly. Equally unexpectedly, no one stepped forward to run as the Democratic candidate to replace him. Except, that is, for an unemployed Marxist whose highest occupational achievement had been as a clerk in the local small town train freight station. And he had been fired from that job for giving out communist literature.

Eager to shape public policy, he stood for election as a commissioner of insurance. A surprising Democratic tidal wave that election year swept him into office. He took the oath of office in jeans and pledged solidarity with the toiling masses.

But one day, a national insurance company launched a tender offer for an insurance company headquartered in his state. A careful reading of North Dakota law made clear that the commissioner of insurance was required to give approval before the deal could begin.

This commissioner was not without the freight of ideological baggage. He believed that insurance companies headquartered in the state ought to be statized. Not nationalized, but statized.

Who's Next?

"[T]he AGs of NAAG, emboldened by their tobacco victory, are already developing a new check list of potential lawsuits that include not just gun manufacturers and the one-time makers of lead-based paint, but HMOs, pharmaceutical firms, nursing home operators, car rental companies, and sweepstakes distributors. Even Hollywood is a potential target, given its violent entertainment. 'No company is too big. No industry is exempt,' says Attorney General Moore, who adds in an aside that, 'Companies that have done nothing wrong and are good corporate citizens have nothing to fear.'[3] Unless perhaps they fall afoul of the definition of 'good corporate citizens' that Mr. Moore and his colleagues have developed. 'There's no question that the state AGs are wielding tremendous power these days through civil litigation,' Tommy Wells, chairman of the American Bar Association's Litigation Section, told the *Dallas Morning News*. 'They are a throwback to the activist agenda of making social change through the court system.'[2.5]

He was not among the number of the economists who believed consolidation could improve economic efficiency. Foreign capitalists to his lights were even worse as a breed than the local variety. And he was not amused.

The tender offer was, for all practical purposes, over.

But the problems caused by the species *barracuda status regularius* do not vanish with the extinction of the largely hypothetical trotskyite state office holder, a truly endangered species. Even the more conventional state attorney, of a type thick as the cod off Newfoundland, can get joy out of an unexpected attack. And the nature of such an attack is not always predictable.

What excites the state attorney general may be a longstanding and time-honored commercial practice. Everyone does it. No sirens sound, no internal warnings blare, when the company does it. But suddenly, surprisingly, in the glare of a well-publicized state investigation, it can become a cause celebre overnight.

For years financial institutions have used customer lists to determine sales of specific products or services of collateral products. They have also discretely marketed such lists to marketers of various kinds. Some banks have also sold data on credit worthiness to marketing firms.

The idea of Big Bank and plutocratic marketeers profiting off the personal information of innocent consumers is the stuff that can stir the appetites of state attorneys general.

Minnesota Attorney General Mike Hatch took the first bite. He went after a major bank holding company. The first morsel was succulent. The bank agreed quickly to a $500,000 payment to the state of Minnesota and $2.5 million to charities in order to settle the case.

The sight of that blood in the water turned other attorneys general to a feeding frenzy. California began to investigate. One problem faced by California Attorney General Lockyer was that there appeared to be no law against the practice. He lamented, "we are investigating. It's not clear yet whether there is adequate law to prosecute criminally or civilly for the sale of private financial information from customers. If the law is inadequate, it ought to be strengthened."

The lack of law did not deter other attorneys general. The attorney general's office in Vermont investigated. One of its staff assistants then became the leader of the national task force on the issue. Soon investigative demands were dropping onto desks in financial institution reception areas from coast to coast.

It is said that someone who wants to attract bees has need only to set out an open vessel full of honey, wait for a lone bee to find the honey, and cover the vessel until that bee has fully satisfied itself. Then let the bee fly away, assured that he will come back to the place where he has found the honey, this time with a swarm of its colleagues.

The same is true of state regulators. If one finds honey in a commercial practice, however time-honored or apparently legal, a success in extorting settlements from the company will be quickly shared with other attorneys general. Before you can say the word "politics," all will be filling themselves with honey, satiating themselves from the sweetness of the polls if not from the pecuniary results of the investigations.

Mazda Motor Corp. America had been aggressively marketing its leasing program for new automobiles. And it promised "penny down" and "no down" terms. One might assume that a consumer would interpret that language to mean that there would be no down payment required to lease a new Mazda vehicle. The customer might well expect there to be certain fees or security deposits or other charges in connection with the lease.

But that is not the way the California attorney general saw it. Since customers in fact were required to pay a variety of fees and payments in connection with the processing of the leases, some of them as high as $900 in total payments, the California attorney general was offended. He brought an action.

"Cut Them in on the Deal"

"U.S. Senator Jeff Sessions, the predecessor to Alabama Attorney General Bill Pryor, recalls that in 1996 he was approached by a group of attorneys who wanted him to hire them to sue the tobacco companies on a 25 percent contingency fee. After Mr. Sessions told them they didn't have a good legal case he recalls, 'they persisted and told me certain names that they wanted to participate...and the person making the proposal to me...was the Lieutenant Governor of Alabama who was a part-time (public official) and a lawyer. He was coming (to see me) as a private attorney, and he was going to make part of the fee out of the case.' After Mr. Sessions objected, he was told 'You can hire some of your buddies, your Republican law firms—cut them in on the deal. Why don't you do that, Jeff. That will be fair, won't it?' Senator Sessions now says he wasn't the only attorney general who had this experience. 'They (went) around the States...approaching attorneys general with this kind of pitch.'"[2.6]

Before long, 21 other states joined in. Mazda decided to settle. It paid $857,000 to state attorneys general in fees and other administrative costs. What Mazda had viewed as an innocent piece of understandable marketing had become a multi-million dollar issue, when Mazda's own attorneys fees and diversion of energies were taken into account.

The appearance of protecting local interests, and especially local consumers, is enough to galvanize your average attorney general into enthusiastic striking. The resources of a state agency are large enough, and the range of state remedies scary enough, that most companies faced with such investigations settle. They roll over for consent decrees.

"Most recognize the enormity of our accomplishment and thank us for achieving so much for the state."[2.7]

—Houston Attorney John Eddie Williams, deflecting criticism of the $3.3 billion that Texas trial lawyers siphoned off from the tobacco settlement.

They figure that if they do not have to admit wrong, and the costs of settlement are not in excess of the costs of defense, they might as well settle, swallow hard, take the bad publicity, and go back to the activity they are best at—making money.

The state attorneys general do not, of course, always win. Like most bullies, they hope they can scare off an opponent before they have to show their strength in battle. And while it is difficult to argue with a strategic decision to settle when settling is cheaper than fighting, there are times when principle matters. In such cases, it is important to know that the most popular of political figures has to sit at the same oak counsel table as his corporate opponent.

In the late 1990s the Minnesota Twins found themselves in much the same position as the Milwaukee Braves of two decades earlier. The Twins had had a remarkable worst to first transformation under the ownership of Carl Pohlad only a few years after moving into a new domed stadium called the Hubert H. Humphrey Metrodome.

That stadium had been designed for football. It had been designed especially for the Minnesota Vikings, a notably successful franchise in getting into the Super Bowl, and a notably unsuccessful franchise in winning the Super Bowl. But the team had used its considerable fan loyalty and general popularity to entice the local public officialdom and the local business community into supporting a new domed stadium. As an afterthought, the Twins were asked to share the stadium. After some concessions were worked into the lease, the Twins agreed.

In the seventh year in the new facility, the Twins' ship came in. With young players like Kirby Puckett, Kent Hrbek, Gary Gaetti and pitchers like the grizzled veteran Bert Blyleven and the young stylist Frankie (Sweet Music) Viola, the Twins came out of nowhere to shock

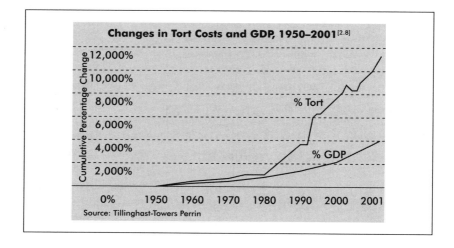

Changes in Tort Costs and GDP, 1950–2001[2.8]

Cumulative Percentage Change

12,000%
10,000%
8,000%
6,000%
4,000%
2,000%
0%

% Tort

% GDP

1950   1960   1970   1980   1990   2000   2001

Source: Tillinghast-Towers Perrin

the baseball world in 1987. First they won their division, then the pennant. Then they won the World Series.

The unleashing of emotion among the phlegmatic Swedes and Norwegians of Minnesota, starved for any world title, burst out dangerously. Fans mobbed the motorcade as the Twins celebrated their World Series victory.

The success of any small market franchise is, alas, typically not sustainable, but the Twins came back in 1991 and won the World Series yet again. Playing in a World Series that Sports Illustrated called the greatest of all time, the Twins reignited local partisans as they won in most exciting fashion, most of the games terminating with a run scored on the last play of the game. Game six saw Kirby Puckett rob the Atlanta Braves of a home run, reaching over the fence to make a circus catch, and then in the bottom of the eleventh rocket the ball into the left-field seats to win as exciting a sixth game as had ever been seen in baseball annals. The fiercely competitive Jack Morris then walked to the mound 10 times in a ten-inning shutout to seal a 1–0 victory in the seventh game. Morris had overruled his manager who wanted to take him out an inning earlier. Again, it was bedlam in victory-starved Minnesota.

But as with Milwaukee a generation earlier, the realities of the small market set in. The sight lines of the dome were not getting any better. The team suffered as salaries escalated. The Pohlad family lost money, year after year. Notwithstanding their long-term loyalty to the area, the ownership of the team was on the brink of making a difficult decision.

It needed either a new stadium that would recognize the financial realities of baseball, or the team would have to leave town. Given the prospect of imminent litigation, I was retained to represent the Twins.

The controversy heated up quickly. The owner of the Metrodome, the local sports commission, sought to deny provisions in the lease that appeared to give the Twins an early "out" from their lease obligations when certain conditions were met. In litigation that was nasty, brutish and short enough to please Thomas Hobbes, we won a quick victory. The Twins could move if they wanted to.

Smoke Screen

"States that are seeking to recover Medicaid fees for smokers from tobacco companies have used trial lawyers to handle their cases. This has led to disputes over breathtaking fees.

"Kansas Attorney General Carla J. Stovall (R.), for example, selected two out-of-state firms to represent Kansas in its tobacco suit. Then she picked her former law firm, Topeka's Entz & Chanay, to be local counsel. Entz & Chanay was to receive $196 million in fees, the final amount to be set by arbitration.

" 'How many hours did you put in on this?' Reader's Digest asked partner Stuart Entz.

" 'We have no way of knowing,' Entz replied. His contract contains this caveat:

" 'Counsel are not required to maintain time records.'

" 'That's bizarre,' says Kansas State Rep. Phil Kline. 'As an attorney I have never been in a circumstance where we didn't maintain records.' Reader's Digest tried to ask Stovall about this, but she declined repeated requests for an interview." [2.9]

But into the controversy came Hubert H. Humphrey II, Minnesota's Attorney General. The son of an illustrious father, whose name still graces the Metrodome, "Skip" Humphrey served an extensive list of civil investigative demands ("CIDs") on the Twins, several other major league baseball teams, Commissioner Bud Selig, the American League, and the National League, and probably, given the temporal reach of the demand, would have tried to subpoena Judge Kennesaw Mountain Landis, if he had been available.

The CIDs were burdensome. They asked for voluminous information. They sought data going back decades, not just years. The authors were curious about reports in the media of some "conspiracy" among the owners to extort a new stadium from the good people of Minnesota in favor of a "billionaire" owner.

State attorneys general have wide latitude in framing civil investigative demands. They are allowed to run free. They are allowed to go on fishing expeditions. That is the nature of their bureaucratic prerogative. Most entities face that kind of investigation with the enthusiasm of someone entertaining the curiosity of a proctologist. They conclude it will be painful, humbling, but necessary to allow the exploration.

The traditional approach is simply to seek to convince the government to modify (or "lim") the demand in order to make it more palatable. State attorney generals expect such a phone call. The extent and breadth of the response is generally negotiable. Here the issue was whether there was a violation of the state antitrust law. It might seem prudent by application of this conventional wisdom to comply with the requests and then to use the facts produced in discovery to argue the attorney general out of the antitrust lawsuit. And, at least as a first resort, try to go along in order to get along.

The subject matter of the CIDs in this instance, however, raised an interesting issue. Did the state have any business seeking to enforce the antitrust laws against a baseball team in the first place? Even if they found some violation after reviewing the responses to the CIDs, did they have any right to prosecute it?

Baseball, after all, was no ordinary business in this regard. Baseball had long been the only sport to have a special exemption from the operation of the federal antitrust laws. In what many critical commentators believed was not Justice Oliver Wendell Holmes' finest hour, he had opined on behalf of the Supreme Court that the federal antitrust laws should have an exemption for major league baseball. That exemption had been twice affirmed by the United States Supreme Court, although with changing explanations for it, since that time.

The most recent case, an early 70's controversy triggered by a lawsuit brought by Curt Flood, had some potential ambiguities. In an

Next Up to Bat

"After tobacco and guns, paint manufacturers have been the next industry to be targeted by trial lawyers. Lead paint stopped being commonly used in American homes in the mid-1950's and was banned by the federal government in 1978. But trial lawyers hope they can make a fortune in class-action suits and state-sponsored litigation against former lead paint manufacturers. So far, lead paint companies have never lost a case, since plaintiffs have been unable to establish that any single defendant produced the 40-year old paint that may have injured a particular person. However, in March 1999, the Louisiana Court of Appeals allowed lawyers representing 2,000 children to sue lead paint makers, the first class action allowed." [2.10] opinion written by Justice Blackmun, which some litigants had sought to exploit, Justice Blackmun had affirmed the federal antitrust exemption in supporting baseball's reserve clause. But some argued that in maintaining the exemption for the reserve clause, the Supreme Court was refusing to apply the exemption to the "business of baseball" generally.

The Flood opinion seemed clear in its affirming of past precedents. Nowhere in the decision did the Court overrule the federal antitrust exemption as it applied to the business of baseball. But rationalizations multiply when courts decide it is time to change a precedent. And the antitrust exemption seemed increasingly to be at risk.

The attorney general of the state of Florida, Mr. Butterfield, had successfully argued in the admittedly cozy confines of his own state court system, that the federal antitrust exemption no longer existed outside the four corners of the baseball reserve clause. The issue had come up in the context of a decision by a major league franchise not to move to the Tampa-St. Petersburg area. Although the case ultimately settled, it had established a precedent.

In the same controversy, Judge Padova in Pennsylvania federal District Court had ruled the same way. He had concluded that the federal antitrust exemption was no longer viable as applied to the business of baseball. That holding had implications for state antitrust regulation as well. If the federal exemption was gone, it followed that any state exemption was gone. The reason lies in a legal doctrine called *in pari materia*. State courts interpreting state laws that parallel similar federal provisions frequently decide to interpret them in the same way the federal courts interpret the applicable federal law. That is interpretation in pari materia. That is what the Minnesota courts had done in the application of state antitrust law. Federal and state antitrust law in Minnesota were interpreted by Minnesota courts in the same fashion.

Friends in High Places

"In Spring, 2000, market share liability legislation was again introduced in the Maryland General Assembly, this time having as its target the one-time makers of lead-based paint. The legislation is expressly designed to help Peter Angelos win his two lawsuits pending against former lead paint makers." [2.11]

Face to face with our politically popular barracuda, we decided to bite back. We immediately launched a civil action on behalf of all Major League Baseball challenging the civil investigative demands. If in fact

Splitting the Company Isn't Enough?

Nineteen state AGs are allied with the federal government in an antitrust suit against Microsoft. (The states and the Justice Department originally filed separate suits, which courts later consolidated.) But there's some evidence that the state AGs want to pursue a more radical solution than the federal government. According to the New York Times, several AGs, including those of New York, Minnesota, Utah, and Ohio, are hoping that the courts will declare that each copy of the Microsoft Windows operating system sold in their states is a separate antitrust violation, which would force Microsoft to pay a fine ranging from $2,000 in Kentucky to $100,000 in New York for each copy of Windows sold. "With per violation or occurrence, that could amount to millions and millions of dollars," said assistant West Virginia AG Doug Davis.[71] [2.12]

baseball had a federal antitrust exemption, it had a state antitrust exemption. If it had a state antitrust exemption, the state Attorney General had no right to bring an antitrust complaint. If the Attorney General had no right to bring an antitrust action, he had no right to seek to discover information relevant to such a potential antitrust action. All the major league baseball parties refused to turn over anything, giving not even name, rank or serial number to Attorney General Humphrey.

The case came on for hearing before Judge Margaret Marrinan, a District Court judge with a good reputation in St. Paul, Minnesota. She heard arguments. She read the briefs. Then came the decision. She joined what she thought to be a trend of decisions by agreeing with Judge Padova. She ruled that the civil investigative demands were appropriate but allowed for negotiation between the parties on how extensive the inquiries should be. She also stayed her order so that it could be appealed.

Here was a chance to negotiate a rather minimal initial response. The strategy needed to be reexamined. Would it be prudent to roll over? We thought we had a principle worth defending. We decided to continue to strike.

We went up to the Court of Appeals. We needed to convince the court to take discretionary review. Appellate courts normally do not intervene in a matter until it is finally decided in the court below. When there is a final judgment, then and only then is it time for appellate review. But that doctrine has various nuances that allow for interim review. There is usually a process to seek a discretionary review while the case below is still pending.

Discretionary review should have been forthcoming here. The ruling of Judge Marrinan had finally concluded the case we had brought in the district court. The only purpose of the action was to quash the CIDs and to avoid compliance with them. She had rejected our argument and had ordered us to comply with them once they had been appropriately refined. Because the case in District Court was only about whether or not the civil investigative demands needed to be answered, the ruling by Judge Marrinan meant that the issue had been decided. And finally.

The Court of Appeals did not see it that way. It decided instead that the appeal was premature. The ruling left the litigants scratching their heads. The lower court action was not, after all, an antitrust action. There would be no ultimate ruling on the merits in that action. It was only about quashing the civil investigative demands. There was nothing more to do. Nothing was premature. If nothing was done, the ruling stood. The issues were resolved. We lost.

The question again was whether to adjust the strategy, go back to district court, and negotiate the terms of the subpoena. Again we opted for an aggressive strategy. We went to the Minnesota Supreme Court.

It was necessary to convince the Minnesota Supreme Court that it should take the case in its discretion and then disagree both with the district court's result and with the appellate court's decision that review of that district court holding was premature. The Supreme Court, whatever its wobbliness in other baseball matters, agreed to take the case.

A full argument was held in the lovely Supreme Court courtroom in the Cass Gilbert-designed Capitol in St. Paul. The Court was indeed curious about the merits. The courtroom was full of interested parties and the press. There was live television. The matter was of intense political interest. The case was covered in the front pages of the local newspapers.

The argument all agreed went well.

Two months later the aggressive strategy had been vindicated. The Supreme Court unanimously ruled against Attorney General Humphrey. It clearly vindicated the antitrust exemption. It became the most persuasive state supreme court precedent showing the continuing viability of the exemption. Major league baseball, and the other recipients, would not have to answer even one of the CIDs.

For the first time in recent memory, a state Attorney General had been denied the right to ask even one question of a corporate citizen of the state. A humbled Attorney General Humphrey sought a long-shot review by the United States Supreme Court. The Supreme Court denied his writ for certiorari.

Major League Baseball advised all of its owners, citing the decision as the best precedent yet in the continuing war to preserve the special benefit the law had given to the nation's pastime.

As often is true, according to the old axiom, God seems to favor the bold.

Chapter 3

This Agency Has Sharp Teeth

It arrives in the morning mail. The letter may look insignificant to the inexperienced executive, like the little cloud no bigger than a man's hand, that Elijah saw. But little clouds and little letters can be ominous. And when this little cloud is heading your way you had best pay close attention.

The letter comes from an agency called the SEC. The acronym stands officially for the Securities Exchange Commission. Its lineage dates to the Roosevelt administration in the 1930s.

The go-go 1920s had roared. Those were days of loose living and easy prosperity. A strong stock market provided fuel for diverse energies. But like all speculative booms, it was not to last. The opiate dream ended with a crash. The collapse of 1929 ended the good times and soon a series of bad policies, Smoot Hawley tariffs, and a shrinking money supply plunged the nation into the Depression.

> One out of eight companies listed on the New York Stock Exchange have been accused of fraud. Already, half of the high-technology companies in the United States have been sued. [3.1]

The election of Franklin Delano Roosevelt launched a new era of activist government. Agencies began to multiply like rabbits. A dismal economy brought forth public policy adventuring and government experimentation.

One of the areas of early government activism was regulating the sale of securities, a reaction to the stock market excesses of the 1920s. The sight of investors leaping off tall buildings, and the stories of lost savings and personal bankruptcy caused by buying up investments that turned out to be little more than "blue sky" from unscrupulous promoters led to a series of laws creating new rules of the road for the securities industry. The first law passed was the Securities Act of 1933. It regulated the issuance of new securities. It had a distinctive regulatory philosophy. Rather than regulate the

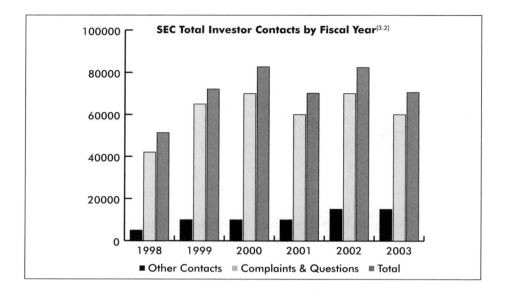

securities marketplace in traditional fashion, the law emphasized disclosure. An efficient market operates well based on prompt and accurate exchange of material information. The philosophy underlying the Securities Act was to command buyers and sellers to be accurate in the representations they make in connection with the purchase or sale of securities.

The 1933 Act was followed by the 1934 Securities Exchange Act. In governing transactions in the aftermarket, the 1934 Act sought to prohibit manipulative practices and fraudulent devices that had been altogether too common in the rip-roaring marketplace of the '20s. The underlying philosophy was again one of disclosure. The law was designed to make sure to the extent it is possible that there is accurate and complete information disseminated to those in the marketplace, in the confidence that the marketplace would then take care of the rest.

A new agency was created to implement and oversee these laws. The Securities Exchange Commission was designed to develop and enforce regulations to carry out the provisions of the 1933 and 1934 Acts. It was given a panoply of remedies. Like the Hoplite of the Roman legions, it was fully armed. It was provided some intimidating weaponry. The intent was to provide all the equipment necessary to search out and destroy fraudulent and manipulative practices in the securities industry. It did so, and does so, in two ways. First, there are required

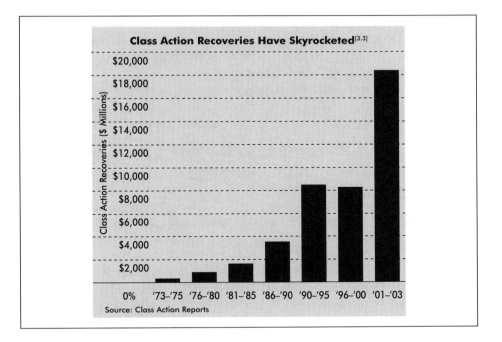

filings that must be made with the agency by public companies. Some are routine. Quarterly and annual disclosures of material information are filed with the SEC. There are also special filing requirements on the occasion of some material change in the condition of the company or in the ownership of its shares or from other triggering events. Second, there is the enforcement arm of the agency, the federal cops on the securities beat, who seek to enforce the requirements of the laws by bringing actions against wrongdoers, sometimes with daunting sanctions, some lethal for careers and reputations.

The letter from the agency, referred to above, looks innocent enough. The reader is informed that the government has begun an informal investigation. It seeks information of two kinds. The government wants to collect documents, and the government wants to interview witnesses. The reasons underlying the request may be various. Perhaps insiders at the company have traded shares of company stock shortly before what appears to be a material event. The stock has taken a hit. It has dropped in value. The sensitive SEC radar notes that shortly before the skid, someone at the company, someone on the inside, has sold shares. The SEC is curious what the insider knew that the outside world didn't, and when he knew it. Or the company has experienced a run-up in share price and shortly before that run-up, an insider has acquired shares. The radar has beeped again. What did the insider know, and when did he know it?

Or the question may relate to revenue recognition. A company is desperate to meet market expectations with respect to its projected earnings and projected revenues for the quarter. Despite significant obstacles, the company's concerted efforts at the end of the quarter appear to have been rewarded. Favorable earnings reports coming from favorable revenue numbers fuel an upsurge in the price of the stock. Those favorable tides in turn are used to give a lift to rewards given to insiders: bonuses to executives, together with lavish stock options. But the SEC is curious again. Was the revenue recognized properly? Was it really revenue? Did the company cut corners to make itself look better than insiders knew was the case?

> "These people fly around in bigger jets than we do. This is no longer a cottage industry."[3.4]
>
> —Robert W. Pike, executive vice-president and secretary at Allstate Insurance, on class-action attorneys.

Or maybe the SEC is interested in selective disclosures made by the company to others outside of its inner circle. It is common, and expected, for executives to talk periodically with analysts who follow the company's stock. This is one way of keeping the market informed of progress the company is making toward achieving its earnings objectives. Earnings are, of course, of critical importance. One way of ascribing value to shares is by a price earnings ratio. If one knows the earnings of a company and assigns a proper multiple to those earnings, one can, with some confidence, fig-

Beware Market Crashes

"Online brokerages are 'probably' financially responsible for computer outages that leave their customers unable to trade," said Securities and Exchange Commission Arthur Levitt. Executives at online trading firms, reports the New York Post's Jesse Angelo, "are terrified of lawsuits from customers claiming they lost money due to computer glitches. E*Trade has already been slapped with such a suit by an Ohio woman who attributes $40,000 in losses to computer problems at the online trading site. The suit seeks class-action status."[3.5]

Not Bad Work If You Can Get It. . .

Securities-fraud kingpins Melvin Weiss and Bill Lerach were recently forced to reveal, during a trial in Chicago, that they earned an average of about $12 million a year apiece from 1994 to 1998. Many of the more successful TV and billboard legal personalities make $2 million to $5 million annually.

Those sums dwarf the earnings of most corporate defense attorneys. In Altman Weil Inc.'s 2000 survey of Law Firm Economics, plaintiffs' contingency firms were shown to have more net income per lawyer ($365,941) than any other specialty, including commercial litigation ($282,733), intellectual property ($190,944), and labor ($189,226). [3.6]

ure out what the price of the stock should be. The earnings estimates shared with market makers and other important analysts can generate reports to the investment community that will have a significant impact on the value of the shares.

But it is tempting to share that information selectively. Rather than putting out a press release or putting it on the business wire, individuals at the company may choose to engage in conference calls with various analysts. To the extent information is casually added to the mix in those conversations and new material data is shared with a small segment of those following the company, such conversations may be viewed as providing special inside information contrary to the securities laws.

Whatever the subject of interest to the SEC, the letter signaling the beginning of an informal investigation—or even more a letter stating that the SEC has embarked on a formal investigation—needs to be taken seriously. In the former case, an "informal" investigation where there has been no formal order, statistics tell us that enforcement action is likely. In the latter case, the case of a formal investigation, enforcement action is virtually assured. And in either case, the enforcement activities of the SEC will always be expensive for the company and its insiders and will inevitably be greeted with fear and loathing by those familiar with the tools of the trade the SEC can brandish, and the draconian remedies the SEC can administer.

Draconian is none too strong a word for what the SEC can do. It can refer a matter to federal prosecutors, since most securities violations can, depending on the use of government discretion, be looked at either as civil or criminal wrongs. A referral to criminal authorities means the case caption will be the United States vs. You. That is always a mismatch. It can lead to executives being taken out of their offices in handcuffs, treated as common criminals, and bundled off on a more permanent basis from business, home and family to languish in a federal prison camp.

While criminal referrals are the worst result, they are not in these days a terribly rare result given the popularity of white-collar crime enforcement. Nor are they the only bitter pill in the SEC medicine chest. The SEC can order a disgorgement of profits from insider trading. The disgorgement typically involves not merely the return of any ill-gotten gains, but an equivalent amount as a penalty, sometimes called a "one time" disgorgement.

> Between 1997 and 2000, American corporations reported a 300% increase in federal class actions and a 1,000% spike in state class actions filed against them. [3.7]

But it is not limited to a one-time multiplier. It can be twice or three times the gain, and it can amount to millions of dollars.

The SEC can also enjoin wrongful conduct in the future. The injunction, even though civil, will be a lifelong emblem, worn like the scarlet "A" of Hester Prynne, a permanent reminder of a sullied reputation. An injunction means that a business person is so untrustworthy, and so likely to violate the securities laws in the future, that a federal court had to use extraordinary powers to bar the person from sinning yet again.

The SEC can also bar trading in the company's stock, and bar individuals—sometimes permanently—from pursuing their livelihood. Accountants can be debarred from practicing before the SEC or on behalf of public companies. The SEC can take legal action against public company executives as well. They can bar them from being an officer of public companies in the future. For those whose livelihood depends on that employment, such an order is the death penalty. Correspondence from a hooded executioner should not be treated lightly. As Samuel Johnson once said, the great thing about a hanging is that it wonderfully concentrates the mind.

And so that first letter, so small in size, so gigantic in significance, cannot be ignored. And the elements the SEC needs to prove to accomplish those harsh results are typically watered down from those a private litigant would have to prove as a plaintiff in an analogous private action. Again and again the courts have created special breaks the SEC can take advantage of in proving its case, in addition to special privileges worked into the substantive laws themselves. An easier burden of proof combined with enormous powers and penalties makes the SEC the 800-pound gorilla in a corporation's worst nightmare.

These expansive rights and enormous remedies mean that the SEC can typically snatch some victory even in cases where its position is weak or without substantial merit. The most conventional result in a garden variety SEC case is what is called a consent decree. The SEC and the private party battle for months or years like pit vipers in a contest for leverage. Ultimately, the SEC proposes a consent decree, especially when it has grave doubts it could prove its case in court.

The consent decree is a device by which the private party consents to certain directives, most typically the directives that it not violate in the future its obligations under the securities laws. It agrees not to violate revenue recognition standards, or not to engage in insider trading, or not to do a host of other things the SEC insists on. In most of these cases, again especially where the SEC case is weak, the company is not required to admit it has been wrong in the past. Without admitting or denying SEC allegations, the company can commit not to do any wrongs in the future.

Emulex Fraud: Gotta Find a Defendant

"With the manhunt for the perpetrator of the Emulex fraud [false news report torpedoed company's stock] apparently over, investors burned by the company's $2 billion post-fraud swing are now hunting for someone, anyone, to sue for legal damages. Two lawsuits have already been filed, one against Internet Wire, which originally distributed the bogus press release, and one against both Internet Wire and Bloomberg, the financial news service that sent out a story based on the press release." [3.8]

Such a resolution is face-saving for the SEC. The agency gets a "victory." It is also minimally pinching for the company. It is obligated to do the right thing in the future. The company is, of course, already obligated to obey the law without the additional constraint of a consent decree giving such a direction. So the constriction on future activities, even if there are more precise obligations imposed on a company than the law requires by the SEC in the consent decree, may be slight. The company thus minimizes the risks of a bad outcome in the courtroom and thinks it got a good result too.

But even a consent decree has something of a negative stigma. It can prejudice a career, tarnish a reputation, and suggest to the outside world the old bromide that where there is smoke there is fire. If the SEC has brought a bad action, why not make them prove their case?

Such was our attitude in a matter involving what I will call "ABCD" Corporation, in which I represented the Chief Financial Officer of the company, whom I will call "Bill Olson." Bill was an energetic, competent, intelligent and capable officer of an up-and-coming computer software company. The company had experienced steady and significant growth. Like all public companies, especially those used to aggressive growth, it was important for the company to seek to meet market expectations with respect to its revenues and earnings. Like many such companies, it had the practice of making aggressive projections, and then working hard to meet them.

In the year brought into question by an SEC investigation, things were no different for ABCD. It had made the aggressive projections it normally did. It appeared to the marketplace that the company would meet them. And when the numbers were released, that expectation seemed realized. The company had—through mighty efforts—met its year's expectations in revenue and earnings goals. But what happened next was not expected. The first quarter of the next year was disastrous.

The SEC suspected that the reason the first quarter was so bad was because the company had booked sales it should not have booked in order to accomplish its year-end goals—goals which triggered bonuses, stock options, and other incentives for company personnel. The suspicions of the SEC proved to have been somewhat justified.

Sales officials of the company had apparently engaged in side contracts and secret representations to some of the company customers. Somewhat reluctant buyers were told that they could rescind their commitments to buy company products up to 90 days or more after the beginning of the next quarter. Some had written side deals that memorialized the understanding. When buyers told company salespeople that they needed approval of corporate management because of the size of the order, salespeople booked the revenue anyway, even though it was contingent. There developed in December of the year, as the end of the year was looming, a series of such shortcuts.

The strategy, of course, was deeply flawed. While such contingent sales and loose revenue recognition policies fulfilled market expectations in the short run, they set the company up for devastation the next quarter. Instead of taking a hit at year end, then reversing the company course in the first quarter with strong sales and earnings serving as a trampoline to vault even higher during the next year, this strategy made for a short-lived party, followed by terrible news in the first quarter that took the company's stock downward, in a trend that ended in the dumpster.

The dumpster was the repository for ABCD's stock price. The SEC investigation spared no expense in proving up its case on revenue recognition. It ultimately leveraged the company into a consent decree and a variety of corrective measures to ensure that such practices would not occur, or be tolerated, again.

But it was not enough for the SEC to come after the company. It wanted individuals as well. Chief among them was Bill Olson. As the Chief Financial Officer of the company, he had a responsibility to oversee financial controls. Revenue recognition was one of the financial matters under his general aegis of the CFO. He became a natural target of the SEC investigative efforts.

But the truth was Bill Olson did not know what the sales force was doing. He did not know because he was not told. His ignorance of the side agreements was not the product of negligence on his part. The evidence began to show that sales people at the company consciously withheld information from him. They did not, as they were required to do, send him side agreements or other contingency documentation.

They did not disclose to Bill Olson what they were doing because they knew that if he knew, the revenue would not be recognized. It is a CFO's worst nightmare: management override of company financial policies, combined with a cover-up so effective that those in the financial function are navigating blind through rocky seas.

Even though the facts suggested that Bill Olson was innocent of any knowing misconduct, the SEC wanted to inflict some pain. They proposed a consent decree. The choice was simple: sign the consent decree, with no admission of wrongdoing, or face the risk of a lawsuit which could end his career as a CFO with public companies if the judgment barred him permanently from such a role as a violator of federal securities laws. The teeth of the barracuda looked very sharp.

Bill Olson decided to bite back. We refused to sign the consent decree. The SEC brought its federal action.

The SEC was not amused by Bill Olson's determination. When he was quoted in the *Wall Street Journal* expressing disagreement with the merits of the SEC action, I got a phone call from the SEC's head of enforcement. With him on the line were five or six of his minions. When one deals with the SEC, one quickly learns that there is no such thing as a private conversation. While a private party often has only one lawyer on the line, the SEC has, it seems, a minimum of two, and more likely three, and sometimes, as in this case, five or six.

The SEC was outraged that Bill Olson had been publicly critical of the SEC in the *Wall Street Journal*. The SEC demanded that he cease making comments to the press. They waited for my response.

"You guys," I said, "have a great deal of power, a great deal of discretion. I honor your office. But nowhere in the 1933 or 1934 Acts do I see any grant to you or your agency of a power to disable the First Amendment. My client has an absolute right to exercise free speech. I agree with what he said and how he said it. He will continue to say whatever he thinks right to say no matter how critical of your agency. Frankly, I think he was kind."

The muttering and sputtering tremulated in the ether as the conversation terminated.

After a period of discovery, the case was ready for trial before a United States District Judge. The SEC was taking the matter seriously. Their chief litigation counsel joined four other SEC lawyers in the court room. The SEC was sparing nothing. It did not want to lose this case.

Stolidly, in a characteristically self-righteous way, they methodically sought to prove up their case. They called Bill Olson for cross examination and sought to bully him on the stand. They called other witnesses who had already been intimidated by their power.

But the judge looked uncomfortable. At one point, he quickly closed his trial notebook and called a hasty recess. I thought I knew why. So did the SEC. "Why do you suppose the judge looks irritated?" I asked.

The SEC lead counsel smiled confidently. "If you don't know, I would be very worried if I were you." The case continued.

When the SEC rested its case, I moved to dismiss. Motions to dismiss at the end of the SEC case are rarely granted. They are rarely granted because they are a stinging rebuke to an agency with a large budget and significant discretion. A dismissal suggests the case genuinely had no merit. The result is not a loss, but a total rout. When I made a brief argument, the SEC responded with scorn. Obviously they had made their case, they said. Obviously they had met their burden.

The judge heard both sides out. He then called a recess.

Twenty minutes later he reemerged. He announced the case was being dismissed. He then read a prepared opinion into the record.

It was seismic in its significance. Not only did the court dismiss an action without the necessity of a defense. Not only had the court already prepared a well-written, well-crafted opinion detailing the reasons why. The court said that it could "not condemn too harshly" the actions of the SEC in bringing the action.

The court also made a specific finding, using a term of art related to the Equal Access to Justice Act signifying that the court found the SEC case to be without substantial merit and allowing us to move for attorneys fees. It was the piece d'resistance, the addition of insult to injury.

We brought the motion. The SEC fought mightily. The motion was granted. The SEC would be ordered to pay over $200,000 because of the weakness of its case. Even though the recovery under the Act was later vacated (it turned out that an insurance company was standing behind Bill Olson and therefore he did not technically meet the financial criteria of the Act), the finding that the actions of the SEC were without merit was not disturbed.

Again, it was time for the man to bite the dog, the snorkeler to nip the barracuda. Bill Olson turned down the option of a consent decree. He insisted on his right to free speech, his right to total vindication of his professional integrity, and his right to rub his antagonists' faces in it.

His choice of principle over pragmatism had paid off.

Chapter 4

Barracudas You Used To Know (and Swim With)

It was a sad story from one of the nation's oldest zoos. The Bronx Zoo at one time set the standard for those who wanted to see exotic animals. Its residents were regularly featured in *Our Weekly Reader*, the weekly newspaper for elementary school students. Its elephants showering themselves on a steamy summer day made the feature page in the Saturday afternoon newspaper.

And although it has been supplanted by more enviro-friendly zoos throughout the country and throughout the world, there was probably no place on earth that one got a better view of lions, tigers, and elephants, along with their curious colleagues from all the world's continents, than from the sidewalks and through the cages of the Bronx Zoo.

But there came a tragic story. A woman zookeeper who helped maintain the lion cages was on one of her daily rounds. She had developed, she thought, some mutual respect, indeed some shared affection, with the beautiful beasts. She was the one who brought them their food. She talked with them. She was a familiar face to them, and their leonine heads were familiar to her. She knew them all by name, like so many old friends.

But one day, while arranging their daily load of raw meat at the feeding station within the cage, a lion leapt on her unexpectedly. With one crushing bite, the report was to say, he crushed her head to the size of a dime. She, of course, died instantly.

A highly capable zoologist, and a treasured colleague, she left many admirers; fellow Bronx zoo employees mourned her loss. But she had made one fundamental mistake, one experienced lion tamer was quoted as saying in the *New York Times*: "No matter how well you know them, you never turn your back on one of the big cats."

The same is true of the "cats" in the corporate executive suite. The launching of a new venture is seldom a solitary assignment. A small

Rand Study Shows Asbestos Claims Rise Dramatically; Cost of Claims Filed by 600,000 People Now Tops $54 Billion

"A RAND study issued today reports that more than 600,000 people in the United States have filed claims for compensation for asbestos-related injuries, costing businesses more than $54 billion by the end of 2000. The study reports that 500,000 to 2.4 million more claims could be filed in the years ahead, costing businesses as much as $210 billion more. . . .

"The first wave of asbestos personal injury litigation, beginning in the 1970s, was confined to about 300 companies that processed asbestos or made heavy use of it, such as in shipbuilding. Now the litigation has spread to more than 6,000 companies that represent nearly all types of industries in the United States, according to the RAND report. . . ." [4.1]

group of entrepreneurial personalities come together with a common dream. They have individual gifts and distinctive personalities but they have one thing in common. They want to live out their entrepreneurial dream. They want to build an enterprise that is successful.

The force of that collective vision bonds them together in the early days of the company. It is one-for-all and all-for-one. The thrill of early victories and the agony of intermittent defeats fuses them into unselfish collaboration. The rough edges of friction are smoothed over or ignored in the excitement and the adrenaline rush of starting something from scratch.

But as St. Thomas Aquinas said, there are two things that test a person's character. One is failing in his aspirations. The other is succeeding in them. The same is true of companies. Failure leads to finger-pointing. And potential litigation. Success leads to desire for control of the new successful enterprise.

By a process of survival of the fittest, the smartest, the most cunning, or the most diligent somehow find their way to the top of the enterprise. Some of the promoters languish, believing that their contribution has not been adequately recognized or compensated. That uneasy environment is also a combustible one. All it takes is a spark.

➤ Financial injury cases are the largest single source of punitive damage awards. 45% of punitive damage awards come from such cases. [4.2]

It is not just the minority shareholder, after all, who is the victim of oppression. Minority shareholders, who for want

➤ Throughout the nation, unpredictable punitive damage awards are on the rise. In the past two years, juries have awarded single punitive damage verdicts of $100 million, $167 million and $250 million. [4.3]

➤ A Rand Corporation study showed that the average punitive damage award in California equals $5.7 million. [4.3]

➤ In Texas, the average award comes out to about $6.7 million. Yale Law School Professor George Priest found that one small rural county in Alabama had an average punitive damage award of $12.9 million between 1989 and 1996.[4.3]

of ability or work ethic get pushed into an eddy at the margins of the white water rush of the principal corporate activities, can by skillful use of the law and lawyers oppress the majority.

In a board meeting of a common public company I attended as a young lawyer, surrounded by a gilt edged collection of board members from some of the biggest corporations in America, I saw a thick-skinned legend of entrepreneurship in the midst of a jeremiad to the board. "Why oh why did I ever get involved in a venture with minority shareholders." Dozens of major shareholder cases later, many of which have found their way into my three-volume treatise on the subject, I understood that his lamentation was more than mere whining.

The plight of the minority shareholder is the stuff melodrama is made of. Those who control the corporate apparatus can be made to appear like those villains of old, with waxed mustaches, who delight in nothing more than taking young maidens by force and tying them on to logs headed for the saw, or banishing widows to a penniless existence in their unheated garret, or foreclosing on an impoverished family of ten. The story tells itself and, the plaintiffs' lawyers hope, causes the ultimate finder of fact to hiss out a rebuke in the form of a seven-figure verdict.

There is an element of truth to the melodrama metaphor. A minority shareholder, especially in a close corporation, is always vulnerable to, and often the victim of, oppression. Majority shareholders can use several sources of power. They have information about the company the outside shareholder does not. They can use corporate money to fight their battles. An outside shareholder cannot. They have time on their side. They can do things that may redound to their benefit, and a minority shareholder may not either know or appreciate the significance of those maneuvers until it is too late. Those who are milking the corporate power and perquisites are in no rush to change.

Case Files: It Started Here. . .

Jones v. Ahmanson, 460 P.2d 464 (Cal. 1969)

Action: Jones, plaintiff, brought an action seeking damages for majority shareholders' alleged breach of fiduciary duty and restraint of trade in violation of common and statutory antitrust laws, Cal. Bus. & Prof. Code § 16756.

Background: The defendants were majority shareholders of the corporation in which plaintiff Jones was a minority shareholder. The defendants created a second corporation and offered certain defendant shareholders an exchange of corporate stock. After the exchanges, the second corporation owned 85% of the first corporation's outstanding shares: thus, the majority shareholders of the first corporation became the majority shareholders of the new corporation, and continued to control the original corporation's stock. The new corporation made its first public offering based primarily on book value attributed to the first corporation and enjoyed a rapid rise in stock trading and share value increase in which the first corporation did not share. The second corporation offered to purchase individual shares of the first corporation for a price under book value. When the first corporation's shareholders refused, the second corporation terminated the first corporation's dividends. The first corporation's shareholders refused a proposed stock exchange and filed suit.

Ruling: The lower court dismissed Jones' claim, but on November 7, 1969, the California Supreme Court reversed that decision. The new rule: controlling shareholders owe a fiduciary duty to minority shareholders. [4.4]

Stories of these kinds of oppressive tactics have galvanized legislatures into seeking to change the law to provide more remedies for minority shareholders. There now exists a variety of laws designed to equal the balance of power in the corporation. That has not always been true. Minority shareholders could not sue directly. They could not allege a breach of fiduciary duty.

In the old days, directors had a fiduciary duty only to the corporate entity, not to minority shareholders. Since the California case called *Jones v. Ahmanson*, in the late 1960s, a new trend has been universally established. Majority shareholders owe minority shareholders a fiduciary duty. The fiduciary duty is the highest duty known to the law, as Justice Cardozo said, "the highest punctilio of honor." And those who have a fiduciary duty must measure up to a high standard. They must live up to a standard that requires full disclosure, total candor, and utter

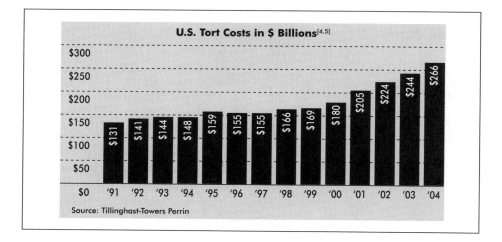

U.S. Tort Costs in $ Billions[4.5]

'91	$131
'92	$141
'93	$144
'94	$148
'95	$159
'96	$155
'97	$155
'98	$166
'99	$169
'00	$180
'01	$205
'02	$224
'03	$244
'04	$266

Source: Tillinghast-Towers Perrin

lack of self-interest or conflict of interest, entire fairness and unblemished honesty. With such a high standard and such a complex of relationships between and among shareholders, the law of fiduciary duty is a fertile source of litigation in this new, minority-shareholder-friendly-environment.

In this new environment, there are now ever more additional remedies. Minority shareholders have long been able to sue on a derivative basis, saying they represent the best interests of the company, and allege that insiders have violated their trust to the company by engaging in corporate waste, by adopting wrongheaded strategies not protected by the business judgment rule, or by engaging in conflicts of interest. If they're successful in assuming the corporate mantle, the minority shareholders can be paid their attorneys fees as well as get other kinds of relief for the corporation, themselves, and their lawyers.

But now there is a more fundamental remedy. Minority shareholders can, under certain circumstances, bring an action for a mandatory buyout. They can seek to buy out majority shareholders, seek to be bought out by the majority shareholders, or seek to have the company put up for sale. In certain cases, they can have the corporation dissolved, even though it is solvent and successful. They can also seek to persuade a court to appoint additional directors or fashion equitable relief to balance the scales of corporate power.

In the appropriate case, these minority shareholder protections work well. But the very existence of these remedies, together with minority shareholders who are embittered and unworthy of corporate

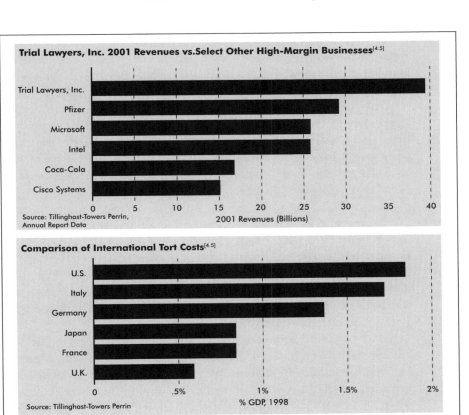

Trial Lawyers, Inc. 2001 Revenues vs.Select Other High-Margin Businesses[4.5]

Source: Tillinghast-Towers Perrin, Annual Report Data

2001 Revenues (Billions)

Comparison of International Tort Costs[4.5]

Source: Tillinghast-Towers Perrin

% GDP, 1998

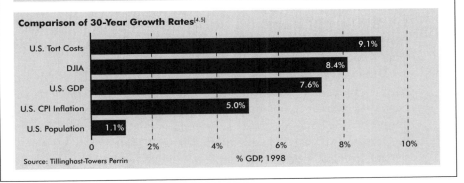

Comparison of 30-Year Growth Rates[4.5]

U.S. Tort Costs 9.1%
DJIA 8.4%
U.S. GDP 7.6%
U.S. CPI Inflation 5.0%
U.S. Population 1.1%

Source: Tillinghast-Towers Perrin

% GDP, 1998

power, aided by the existence of a motivated class of plaintiffs' lawyers, is a dangerous mix.

There is a theory that a corporation faced by such dangers should simply buy its way out of this kind of mischief. But the bee stings of a minority shareholder can accumulate to an allergic reaction that threaten the body of the corporate patient. They are always meddlesome and painful. They are always a nuisance. But unless dealt with, they can sometimes cause corporations to get very sick indeed.

Once the action is engaged, there is an overwhelming motivation to get it settled, even by paying the minority shareholder far more than his action is worth. Too often, one of the initial promoters of the company and a long-term, sometime loyal friend becomes a barracuda with sharp teeth. There is a corporate fragging and an innocent insider is endangered by friendly fire.

Manny Villafaña is a man of immense charm, entrepreneurial talents and energy. Although a cosmopolitan and worldly executive, looking now like a descendant of the Spanish nobility, Manny grew up in the urban jungle of Spanish Harlem in New York City. He successfully navigated his way through the dangerous streets of the city and into the local boys club. Overcoming daunting obstacles, he made his way to a better future by a commitment to education combined with great imagination and diligence.

Manny became famous when he plunged into an emerging field of great social benefit: the application of technology to medicine. Manny's first venture was an effort to market a new product of great potential. It was a heart valve. A new era in medical technology had been launched when Dr. C. Walton Lillehei invented a pioneering heart valve, one that could lengthen life and enhance it for those suffering from diseased hearts. The market potential was apparent. Bringing the product to market required someone with special daring and entrepreneurial zeal. That someone was Manny Villafaña.

Drawing on an intensely personal history, Manny named his company St. Jude after the patron saint of hopeless causes. The heart valve he was to market might supply the hope that had been missing from people whose lives had been shortened and made more difficult by ineffective heart valves inside them. Manny Villafaña became the first person to market one of the most beneficial medical devices ever to hit the marketplace, the heart valve. St. Jude Medical continues to be a remarkably successful company to this day.

There is an inherent restlessness about the entrepreneur, a restlessness that Manny shared. After St. Jude was up and running and became a smashing success, Manny went on to new ventures. Cardiovascular Solutions was another venture he began and saw to stability and prosperity. Full of energy and ideas, Manny loved to find and pursue opportunities for himself, and others. (Indeed, when he gave his name and counsel to one of the nation's top steakhouses, Manny's, he was facetiously accused of an antitrust violation: a purveyor of heart remedies who sells huge porterhouse steaks is obviously seeking vertical integration.)

But the success of his past heart valves did not leave Manny satisfied. A certain percentage of those who received the valves developed strokes that were sometimes fatal. It was a small percentage, but for those who sustained a stroke, it was a 100 per cent calamity. Manny wondered whether the application of technology could eliminate that side effect of otherwise successful heart valves.

Manny founded a company called ATS Medical. The Company had an idea that refined the design of the traditional heart valve. It was to market a heart valve that had a small concavity. There was something about this design that appeared to be effective in protecting the recipient of the heart valve from the risk of stroke. Ahead of ATS Medical was difficult competition with companies with which Manny had been involved in the past. They included St. Jude and Medtronic.

More important than that competition, however, was convincing the FDA to follow its own rules and procedures in the cumbersome approval process. The FDA was often rule bound and bureaucratic. To add a millimeter or two to an already proven and effective catheter might require an additional five years of bureaucratic leaf raking. Such an obstacle course was especially daunting given Manny's knowledge that each year many thousands would die or be disabled by strokes because they could not have a valve that was proving very successful in the elimination of such risks in Europe and other parts of the world.

But there was another obstacle for ATS Medical. It was closer to home. Manny had started the company with the help of three senior officers. They had good résumés and relevant experience. They became part of the founding team of ATS Medical.

But Manny became disappointed with their productivity. He worked with them to see if they could be salvaged. But it was one of those corporate marriages that would not succeed. Notwithstanding the generosity and stock options that Manny had lavished on his colleagues, the insiders felt mistreated. The gang of three, as they were known to others at the Company, decided they had had enough. They sued.

Given the administrative and marketing difficulties of starting a new medical devices company, Manny Villafaña did not need to have an internal civil war. He did not need potentially lethal litigation from people who had been inside the company. The launching of litigation by one of the top shareholder litigation and class action law firms in America was an ominous event. It threatened years of distraction, expense, and hits to the corporate reputation. And, ultimately, it could mean the destruction of the company itself.

Although the plaintiffs and their counsel were open to the quick payoff and were ready to go away, Manny felt that he was in the right. He was not prepared to go quietly into that night. After long conversations on the risk of rewards and of an aggressive defense, we chose to strike back—hard.

Within a week of the filing of the complaint, the three insiders were being deposed. A deposition provides a party to a litigation the opportunity to bring in a witness, ask him questions under oath, have those comments recorded by a court reporter, and thus discover basic facts the other side will be relying on during the course of the litigation. Among the many types of laborious and expensive discovery provided by the rules of civil procedure which govern the course of modern litigation, depositions are the most effective way of getting information, pinning the other side down to a single story, developing contradictions in testimony that can later be exploited, and setting up witnesses for devastating cross-examination in the courtroom.

There is an additional advantage to depositions. When one asks for documents, or when one submits formal questions called interrogatories, the other side and their lawyers are forced to educate themselves on the case. They pore through relevant documents. They carefully craft legalistic inserts that appear to answer the formal interrogatories but really say nothing helpful. They converse about the case, its strengths and weaknesses. By the time the laborious process of responding to interrogatory discovery is over, lawyer and clients have prepared their case. Their basic training is over. Then when the deposition notice comes, the witness understands why the questioner is questioning him in the way he does. He sees the seams. His lawyer knows the documents. Like a well-trained army, the adversary knows the strategy and the armaments of the opponent.

By insisting that depositions happened first, and with blitzkrieg timing, we shortened the time of preparation. The best lawyers, and hence the busiest lawyers, frequently do not prepare for deposition with their clients with as much care as they do document reviews with them. An hour or two in the office reviewing what a deposition is and talking over the basic facts and themes of the case are usually all the party and counsel have time for. And if there are gaps in the preparation of the witness, it shows when the witness is challenged by difficult questions in the deposition.

Getting someone under oath early is not without its dangers. This may be the last chance a court will permit the witness to be deposed. Later documents may raise interesting lines of inquiry that cannot be pursued until trial because one has already had his shot at the witness. The person taking a deposition may not be as prepared to ask sensitive questions as he would be later. The deposition might, that is to say, be premature.

But this seemed like the time for an aggressive biting back at the trio of barracudas. Rapid fire questions, coming from strange angles, caught each of the three off guard. Admissions were made. Critical documents were contradicted. Before the three days of intensive questioning were over, each of the three found themselves tangled up with ropes of admissions, contradictory testimony, and ill-advised responses that they would now have to live with the entire course of the litigation. It was the first round and the bout was over.

The deposition devastation paid off. Their leverage lost, the case on life support, their ability to keep past stock options threatened, the plaintiffs had no choice. They had to settle.

The plaintiffs were ready, after the normal haggling, to walk away from their litigation and take absolutely nothing. They would have to pay their own attorneys' fees. They had taken a bath.

But we wanted something more. We wanted money from them for what now was clearly shown to be an unmeritorious lawsuit. The plaintiffs balked. Their counsel pled for the chance to dismiss their complaint without further consequence. But Manny held firm.

At the end of the day, the plaintiffs had to pay close to one-half a million dollars out of their own pockets, in addition to whatever they paid their sophisticated counsel, simply to drop the lawsuit they had brought. They did it not to acquire anything or to gain anything. They paid for the right of surrendering.

Once the settlement was announced, the newspapers had a field day. The journalistic love for the-man-bites-dog story caused one newspaper to call it an "unusual settlement," pointing out that plaintiffs had been forced to pay hundreds of thousands of dollars for the right to dismiss a lawsuit they had earlier begun. Rather than being paid off, they paid off the defendant.

The general counsel of the company smiled when the checks were delivered. A start-up medical device company is not expected to be profitable for many years. The research and development, the initial marketing efforts, the time-consuming and money-devouring frustrations of dealing with the FDA, and the complexities of the establishment of an international market to provide revenues while the device seeks approval in United States, all cost money. Investors know that. It takes time.

They also know something else. The legal department of the company is not a profit center. It is often viewed as a net drain on corporate assets. Marketing fuels the company revenues. Back office controls are necessary to save the company money in the future. But because the law department makes no widgets and sells no product, it is an expense item on the budget.

For the general counsel and the company called ATS Medical, however, there was a final aspect of the man bites dog story. In the year of the settlement, the law department of ATS Medical was its chief profit center.

The barracudas had been bitten.

November 9, 1993

Star Tribune
It's where you live.

Former Helix officers end up paying

Steve Alexander; Staff Writer

Former officers who were ousted in 1991 from Plymouth-based Helix BioCore, now ATS Medical, have agreed to pay the company $488,750 worth of stock instead of collecting the $2 million they originally sought through a breach-of-contract suit.

The unusual settlement, in which the suing parties wound up paying, occurred after nearly all the claims filed by three former Helix officers were denied in October by Hennepin County District Judge H. Peter Albrecht. At the same time, the company filed $15 million worth of counterclaims against the former executives.

Helix founders John Holroyd and John Salstrom agreed to pay ATS Medical 85,000 shares. . . . [4.7]

Chapter 5

The Right Role in the Melodrama

Before lawyers plied their trade in the courtroom, societies had other ways to resolve conflicts. The most common among them was the ordeal. Because there was no developed methodology for getting at the truth when people had conflicting stories, people resorted to the courtroom of their gods, or "oath deities." These deities were invoked to settle disputes by use of two primordial means.

The most popular trial by ordeal was the water ordeal. Someone accused of wrongdoing would be bound and thrown into the water. If he drowned, that was a conclusive finding by the oath deities that he was guilty. If, however, he bobbed to the surface, that showed he had been vindicated. The methodology was, in a sense, a primitive lie detector. Someone guilty and conscience stricken might well tense up in the water and fall like a rock. Someone who truly believed he would be vindicated, and had a clear conscience, might relax amidst the waves and float harmlessly to the surface again.

Another means of ordeal was the ordeal by fire. The accused would take fire into his hands. If his burns healed naturally, he would be viewed as acquitted. If they got infected, that would be a sign that the oath deities, the ultimate jury, had ruled against him.

These ordeals are also reflected in the Bible. When Israel was in a highly litigious conflict with the Egyptians, each with a champion advocate, Moses or Pharaoh, and each with a client, the God of Israel and the "gods" of the Egyptians, the Red Sea parted for the Israelites, showing their vindication. The Red Sea submerged the legions of Pharaoh, showing their condemnation.

The themes of passing through the water or the fire are frequent in the Bible and other ancient literature. As an old spiritual, one that gave rise to a famous book by James Baldwin, says, "God gave Noah the rainbow sign, no more water, the fire next time."

There were, of course, other forms of ordeal as well. Sometimes a woman accused of infidelity would drink a mixture of ingredients, including dirt on the floor. If she got sick, that would be a sign that her protestation of innocence was untrue. If she remained well, she was to be believed. Here again, there may have been a primitive lie detector at work, since the anxieties of a guilty conscience may well affect the immune system. The medieval ordeal of putting a cracker in a person's mouth and telling him to swallow it in a short period of time might well have had the same impact. The person whose cottonmouth betrayed his guilt, because he knew he was lying, might well have more difficulty swallowing than the person confident of his innocence.

The anthropologist Glickman gives examples from African culture. There he found in one tribe an ordeal closer to the modern courtroom: an ordeal by insult. The two sides of a controversy were evaluated by their ability to frame creative insults. By this quantitative and qualitative ordeal, Don Rickles would be the Clarence Darrow of the continent. Other tribes had clicking rituals based on mouth sounds, joking ordeals, or story contests. Some dissatisfied clients, fresh from drubbings at the hands of juries in our enlightened system, may well look for inspiration to these African models.

But among the most charming of the trials by ordeal was ordeal by champion. Each side would pick a strong man. The two strongmen would battle, perhaps to the death. The one who had made the better choice of champions would be rewarded, validating Ambrose Bierce

"An Affront to Reason"

Barbara Carlisle and her parents claimed that Delaware-based Whirlpool Financial National Bank and Alabama Gulf Coast Electronics had tried to cheat them on the purchase of two satellite dishes. The three signed on to a $34 a month payment plan for terms of four years and four months, but said that they'd been told it was only for three years. Total difference? A respectable but relatively small $1,088.

The jury believed the plaintiffs' story and awarded them a starkly disproportionate $975,000 in compensation. But that dwarfish little first million was just a warm-up. The jury then proceeded to ding the defendants to the tune of $580 million in punitive damages. The Chattanooga Free Press called the award "an affront to reason."

The governor and legislature subsequently enacted tort reform measures, but it is uncertain whether their efforts will endure future judicial scrutiny. [5.1]

and his Devil's Dictionary that tells us that a trial is a contest to see which side has hired the best lawyer. Such a means of dispute resolution removed the clients from the heat of the battle at least until judgment was entered.

A good example of this, though on a national scale, was the battle of Israel vs. the Philistines recorded in the first book of Samuel. Goliath sauntered onto the battlefield challenging any Israelites within earshot to meet him for the ordeal struggle. The stakes were larger than personal pride or an individual's life or death. This was a battle between two nations. The champion battled for his country. If the champion lost, the country lost. A young and unintimidated litigator named David came forward while the other litigation professionals, scared of this particular courtroom, cowered in caves. David won the battle, the hearts of his people, and a great national victory.

The modern courtroom is an outgrowth of the champion ordeal. Each side picks his champion, seeking the best lawyer. The stuff of this ordeal, however, is not water, not fire, and not the sword, staff, or sling of the champion ordeal. And, outside of certain rustic jurisdictions, no crackers are involved.

Nowadays the ordeal of the corporate defendant is what we might call a trial by melodrama. The script writers are those lawyer "champions" who seek to construct a drama along the lines of a somewhat sentimental melodrama, usually with the help of jury consultants who apply the makeup, give tips on the costuming and staging, and help assign the appropriate roles. They cast both sides in familiar roles.

Diva awarded $11M for broken dream

A Little Rock, Ark. jury recently awarded aspiring opera singer Kristin Maddox, now 23, $11 million "for injuries she suffered when an American Airlines jet went off a runway last year while landing in a thunderstorm." Maddox was studying opera in hopes of becoming a star but says damage to her voice box and hands in the crash ruined her professional chances. Her lawyer, "Bob Bodoin, told jurors that no amount of money would make up for her pain and the loss of a career that could have rivaled opera stars Beverly Sills or Luciano Pavarotti's." However, a university voice teacher who evaluated one of Maddox's pre-crash performances on video said she had a voice that, while "lovely," was also too light to fill an auditorium in the Sills or Pavarotti manner. [5.2]

The ultimate design is to provoke a somewhat unsophisticated jury to hiss the bad guys and swoon over the good guys in a classic battle of light vs. darkness. It is power against weakness, legal technicalities against justice and fairness, right against wrong. The young woman is being strapped to a log and sent toward the oversized saw, to be neatly bisected if no one intervenes. Those who put her on the log are apparent, dressed as they are in their black capes and waxen mustaches. They thrill to exercise their power to do wrong. They are the landlords who throw all of the impoverished family into the wintry cold of the streets. They are the rich bankers that send off to debtors' prison those down on their luck. The poor child and widow they delight to squash under the heavy heel of plutocratic power.

But wait, the champion, David-like, appears. He beats back the forces of oppression, unties the ropes that bind the young lady to the log, and saves the day. This champion, of course, is the trial lawyer representing the plaintiff against the evil corporate powers on the other side of the table. For such heroic intervention, it is only right to reward these underdogs lavishly from the corporate treasury.

Most serious people, of course, have little patience for such melodramas. They prefer Shakespeare, or even Arthur Miller. But melodramas have a certain mass appeal. And any defendant who underestimates their appeal may be in for a rude surprise.

Justice or Lottery?

In *Walt Disney World Co. v. Wood*, a woman was injured when her fiancé struck the go-cart she was driving at Disney World. The jury found her 14 percent at fault, her fiancé 85 percent at fault and Disney only 1 percent at fault. But, under the doctrine of joint liability, Disney was required to pay 86 percent of the plaintiff's claimed damages. [5.3]

When the emotive power of melodrama meets a nicely nuanced argument, the melodrama almost always wins. The hidden persuaders stealthily written in the script by experts at evoking emotion can overcome otherwise overwhelming legal and factual arguments. Once the roles are established and the defendant becomes known as Snidely Whiplash, the ultimate conclusion will never be in doubt.

But what is to be done if you do indeed represent the defendant? Do you bring every possible legal motion to dispose of the case and, failing to win them, settle on the courthouse steps before the jury orders

If Henry Ford Had Only Known

Welcome to the new world of assembly-line litigation. Suing Corporate America is a big business.

While there are no authoritative data, a conservative estimate of total annual plaintiff-lawyer income, based on information culled from the Internal Revenue Service, ATLA, and industry consultants, is at least $25 billion. Add the value of the judgments they win for victims and corporate-defense expenditures, and the sum goes much higher. Tillinghast-Towers Perrin, a management consultant with a specialty in insurance issues, estimates that the overall annual cost of the American tort system, including payments to injured people, legal fees, and administrative expenses, was at least $165 billion in 1999. That was about 2% of gross domestic product--twice as much as in most industrial countries. [5.4]

the hooded executioners to lop off your head? Do you relax and assume the jury will be able to see through the pandering and psychological tricks of the adversary? Do you plant seeds of error with the help of a clueless judge on the strength of the assumption that a runaway jury will be reigned in at some level of the judicial system?

None of these techniques is acceptable. Each is dangerous. When you are defending yourself, you are losing. And when you are defending yourself against the charge of being Snidely Whiplash, you are losing badly.

There is a better way. Write the drama yourself. You assign the roles. You take the moral high ground. You convince the jury that the plaintiff and his lawyers are the villains. Let them cheer for you, and hiss for them. It is possible.

Take the case of *Bill Bullet vs. Big Bank and Big Eight*. Bill Bullet was an entrepreneur with a special vision. The defendants were, respectively, "big bank" and "big accountant."

Bullet and his wife gathered their assets to start his dream business, a commercial satellite TV operation. He had acquired expertise in the technology and business aspects of his mission as a professor at a major university. Now, venturing forth from his academic ivory tower, Bill Bullet wanted to build the killer business. Believing that the multiplying of television options could allow him to reinvent himself, and become newly enriched and empowered, he decided he could be at the vanguard of this exploding field.

He carefully teased out his business plan, working side by side with his loyal wife, and developed an idea that he believed would meet the needs of consumers and let him live out the American dream. All he needed was capital. And he knew where he needed to get it. That most intelligent and elusive of criminals, Willie Sutton, famously said it. In answer to the question of a puzzled interviewer who wanted to know why a man with the gifts and talents of Willie would rob banks, Willie replied, "because that's where the money is." And Bullet, knowing where the money was, sought to persuade Big Bank, a huge banking enterprise, to finance his operation. He was persuasive. The bank agreed.

> A jury decided 75% of all tort cases brought to trial in U.S. district courts. A jury trial decided a majority of diversity of citizenship cases (88%) and Federal question cases (63%). [5.5]

> Plaintiffs won 45% of all tort trial cases in which a judgment was known, 44% of personal injury cases, 29% of product liability cases, and 54% of cases involving property damage. [5.5]

Bullet also enlisted the services of a large national accounting firm. Big Eight became his accountant. The stature of that accounting firm would be further evidence of his seriousness and credibility.

Bullet closed on his loan, signing off on the many different forms of financing agreements that were required to give him his seed capital. And he began to work the business, convinced that it, and he, would be successful.

Before he could reach the fulfillment of his vision, however, disaster struck. Due to the insistence by the bank on the performance of certain covenants (written, as their trial lawyers would later have it, by the bank's cunning lawyers into the loan agreements) and his defaults, the bank suddenly called his loan. At the same time, the accounting firm rushed in to see his accounting records, then seized them, effectively putting him out of business, in a maneuver he was later to call "the big heist."

Bill Bullet was out of business. His dream was scattered to the winds. The powerful big cigars of the world of high finance, bankers and accountants, had shut him down and crushed his spirit. And it appeared now that only his lawyers could attempt to balance the scales of justice, to intervene on behalf of him and his wife, and to get his dream restored.

As the jury selection started in the Bullet case, the influence of jury consultants was evident in the curious kind of questions asked of the jury. What color was their favorite color? Had they ever been "squeezed" by someone with more physical or financial power? How did they feel when they had been "squeezed?" How many focus groups, how many consultants, had been gathered to create such questions? Central casting was doing its thing.

It was not difficult to discern how the plaintiffs wanted the script to unfold. The barracudas were looking to take a big bite out of Big Bank, whom I represented. But how was Big Bank to respond? At this point in the proceeding, we could make a technical, and legally impeccable, defense. The Bullets had indeed violated certain loan covenants. The documents did technically allow us to call the loan. We were very sorry that Mr. Bullet was unable to fulfill his lifelong dream, but business is business. There was indeed a "raid" on the business to get documents, but it was justified, and legal.

One could, as I say, make such arguments. One frequently hears them in major litigation. One can make them in a business-like fashion. But don't they sound as though they come from the mouth of Mr. Whiplash? You missed a month's rent, Ms. Widow-Woman, so I can technically tie you to the log.

In melodramas, the bad guys always rely on the technicalities of the lease or a missed payment. The jury expects such dry legalities and expects, at some intuitive level, to blow aside such impediments along the way to doing substantial justice. And they typically break through such legal restraints with the ease of Samson flexing his muscles and breaking the green which he was wound up in by Delilah. As Vince Lombardi once said, the only thing a prevent defense prevents is victories. In this kind of prevent defense, such pettifoggery, however justified by the law, prevents victory and, generally speaking, almost guarantees a huge verdict for Dudley Doright.

It is much better to reverse roles. Make the plaintiffs the villains in the drama and have the jury hiss at them. But how to do so is the question. The two keys to winning this kind of trial by melodrama are the matter and the manner of the defense. The matter is the metaphor. And whoever wins the battle of the metaphor usually wins the game. If the metaphor is Big Bank squashing the entrepreneurial visionary, the bank loses. But alternative metaphors await the scriptwriter.

Ladies and gentlemen of the jury, let's go back to a critical date in this controversy. Sitting at a table in a downtown office were representatives of my client, the bank. Across the table were the two plaintiffs. The bank was there as guardian of its customers' treasured assets. Ordinary people work hard, spend what they need to support their families, and seek to put aside extra money for college educations, for rainy days, for future retirement. They generally entrust this money to banks. The bank needs to show itself a good steward of its depositors' money.

They take these deposits in and invest them wisely so they can secure their ability to return the deposits and pay appropriate interest, as well as make a return for their shareholders.

As the parties gathered around the table that day, the plaintiffs were asking for substantial money, millions of dollars. And the faithful employees of the bank had to decide whether it would be wise to entrust these deposits to these plaintiffs. Each side would be called upon to slide something across the table. The bank would be called upon to push a huge amount of its depositors' money across the table. But what would come back from the other side? What would the plaintiffs give in exchange to the bank for this money?

Promises, ladies and gentlemen. Only promises. Pieces of paper with promises written on them. These promises are called covenants. They would be evidenced by signed agreements. On the strength of the bank's faith that the plaintiffs would be willing to fulfill the promises they made in these documents and live up to the representations, the bank would decide if it could give them all this money. The bank would have to hold

Arsonists Sue for Insurance Benefits After Being Denied Coverage for Damages They Caused to Neighboring Building

Two Alpena, Michigan men set an arson fire in their store with the hope of collecting insurance money. They admitted that they intended to simply have a small, smoky fire that would damage their inventory, which apparently wasn't selling very well, so they could collect on their insurance policy. However, when the fire spilled over into the adjoining store, the men sued the insurance company. They argued that they set the fire in their own store, but that the fire next door was accidental and therefore they should receive coverage for the damage to the other building. A panel of the state Court of Appeals amazingly reversed the trial court's decision to dismiss this ridiculous case, but the Michigan Supreme Court, in a unanimous decision, eventually reversed the Court of Appeals and ruled that the fire "cannot be characterized as an accident." [5.6]

Woman Sues Child After Ice Skating Collision

A 12 year old girl was skating at a public ice rink in Berkley, Michigan when she ran into another skater and knocked her down causing a knee injury to the fallen skater. The injured woman sued the girl. The trial court dismissed the case saying that the child's manner was not reckless. The trial court stated that the accident occurred during an open skating session at the ice rink and that there are certain risks that must be assumed by participants in recreational activities, especially on ice which is in itself dangerous because of its slippery and hard nature. Sadly, a panel of the Court of Appeals reversed the trial court decision and allowed the case to go to trial. Fortunately for the girl and her family, the Supreme Court reversed the Court of Appeals stating that "When one combines the nature of ice with the relative proximity of skaters of various abilities, a degree of risk is readily apparent. . ." [5.6]

these pieces of paper up to the light, look the plaintiffs in the eye, take their measure, and see whether they could be trusted.

In this case, the bank trusted the plaintiffs. They believed that they would keep the promises. With that confidence, they passed millions of dollars across the table. And what they got back were the signed promises of the plaintiffs to do certain things in a certain way to give the bank assurance they would pay the money back on time.

As Shakespeare once said, "untune that string and see what discord follows." He was referring to the world of social and business relationships as an instrument held together by the strings of promise and mutual obligation. And when someone untunes one of those strings and breaks his promise, discord is introduced into all levels of society.

This is a case about broken promises. The bank did what it was obligated to do under the agreement. It did entrust the plaintiffs with its depositors' money. But as we will see, the plaintiffs broke their promises. They untuned the string. This is a simple case about enforcing social promises.

The power of this metaphor is in its grab for the white hat. If someone is to wear the black hat and the black cape, make sure it is the other party.

Once the metaphor is chosen, it is important to stay on message throughout the entire trial. The metaphor is stated, repeated, illustrated and delicately ornamented in every conceivable fashion.

But the manner of presentation must be well linked to the matter of presentation. If in fact the plaintiffs have broken promises, they must be exposed. In the Bullet case, Bill Bullet took the stand. He explained

> There has been a reduction from 12 to 1 in the producers of serum for whooping cough.[5.7]

> There has been a reduction from 20 to 2 in the number of companies willing to produce football helmets intended for any level of play.[5.7]

> Union Carbide funded and developed a suitcase-size kidney dialysis unit for home use, but sold it to a foreign corporation after determining the potential liability risks made the product uneconomical.[5.7]

> Lederle Laboratories, which is now the lone maker of the DPT vaccine (all other manufacturers having abandoned the field) raised its price per dose from $2.80 in 1986 to $11.40 in 1987 to offset the cost of lawsuits.[5.7]

> [I]nsurers are abandoning plaintiff havens, leaving thousands of doctors and hospitals scrambling to find coverage. The country's biggest malpractice insurer, the St. Paul Companies, last year exited the business entirely after incurring nearly $1 billion in losses.[5.7a]

> In Pennsylvania, one of 18 states with out-of-control rates, only two malpractice insurers remain, down from ten only five years ago. In Mississippi, at least 15 insurers have left the market since 1997.[5.7a]

his vision to the jury, gave the frightening story of the big heist, talked about his dreams being dashed. But the jury had heard the opening statement, had been gripped by the metaphor, and was not giving Bill Bullet their entire heart. They were sitting with their hands clasping their pocketbooks, wondering who this plaintiff really was.

When the direct examination was finished, it was tempting to do a normal cross examination. Start out slowly. Highlight some facts. Make a few incidental points. Then gradually pick up the pace and begin to challenge the witness a little more strongly. But given the strength of the metaphor, it seemed to me a more direct assault was called for.

The first question was something like this. "Now, Mr. Bullet, when you told this jury such and such just a few minutes ago, you were telling a bold-faced lie, weren't you?" The smooth and rehearsed performance of the witness while under direct examination was now tested by fire. Not expecting the ferocity of the attack, Mr. Bullet rolled his eyes heavenward, cleared his throat and said, somewhat tentatively, "no." He was then promptly contradicted by a document that seemed to prove conclusively he had indeed testified falsely.

It was downhill from there. This was a Joe Frazier cross examination. Put your head on the chest of the adversary and whale away to the body.

Every time the witness was challenged, he went through the same ritual: glance heavenward, clear the throat, and give a somewhat tentative answer. One of the court personnel, present during the trial, still greets me with a mimicry of the full-day's cross examination—an eye roll, cough and stammer.

Whatever one's assessment of the style points of such a cross examination, it was clear that the jury thought Mr. Bullet was not to be trusted. If the metaphor was the melodrama, Dudley Doright had to show by his manner that this was for him a matter of conviction.

The trial went on for several weeks. When closing arguments were concluded, the defendants staying on message to the end, the jury went out to deliberate. They had 44 complicated questions to answer on their special verdict form. The first task was picking a foreperson. They were then to answer the questions.

They went out of the courtroom that day at 20 minutes to noon, then decided to have lunch. They came back from lunch at about 1:30 PM.

At about 1:45 PM they told the astonished federal marshals that they had already reached a verdict.

On all 44 questions, they decided for the defendants.

Next came post-trial motions. Plaintiffs sought judgment notwithstanding the verdict. It was denied. But we stayed on message. We moved for sanctions under Rule 11, which requires someone initiating a pleading to have a good faith basis in law and fact for the assertions in it. The federal judge found that there had been a

> Each year, more than 7.5 million lives in this country are either saved by implantable medical devices—like pacemakers for heart patients or shunts for hydrocephalus—or improved through products like replacement eye lenses for cataracts and balloon angioplasty devices. Unfortunately, a recent study reveals that at least 75 percent of suppliers of biomaterials used to make medical implants have banned sales to U.S. implant manufacturers. In deciding to sell or not to sell to the implant market, risk of legal liability was a key factor for 100 percent of suppliers. [5.8]

technical violation of Rule 11 by the plaintiffs but did not award sanctions.

We did not wait for them to appeal. We appealed to the Eighth Circuit Court of Appeals on the failure to award sanctions. They appealed the verdict. The Eighth Circuit determined they did not want oral argument on plaintiffs' appeal, but wanted a hearing on our claims under Rule 11. The alarmed plaintiffs' lawyers were forced to retain counsel to represent them, presumably at their expense, while sanctions against them were deliberated. The Circuit disposed of their appeal quickly. The judgment was affirmed. And while they did not choose ultimately to add insult to injury by imposing stiff monetary penalties on plaintiffs' lawyers, the message was clear for all who would listen.

> Trial lawyers are pursuing as many as **120,000 lawsuits against America's 500,000 physicians** at any one time.[5.9]

If you are going to sue the bank, you had better have more than a melodrama. Because the bank is not amused and will pursue the plaintiffs in any way possible. As in judo, where the idea is to use the force of your opponent's assault against him, so in trial by melodrama the emotional force of the plaintiffs needs to be turned against them.

"John Cafe" was a restaurant owner from Nebraska who came to a prominent medical clinic for an examination. Because he had arthritis, he was treated with injections of gold which seemed to mitigate the symptoms.

While going through the normal indignities of medical examination at the clinic, he was given an injection of gold the evening before he was to go back to his home. The nurse brought in three syringes filled with gold.

> The "lawsuit tax" represents as much as thirty percent of the cost of a stepladder, over ninety-five percent of the cost of childhood vaccines, one-third the cost of a small airplane, and actually exceeds the cost of making a football helmet. [5.11]

Cafe was not used to seeing so much gold. He questioned the amount. The nurse told him, in her best bedside manner, to roll over. He obediently complied. She injected the business end of the syringe into the patient's business end.

The next morning when the doctors were reading the charts over morning coffee one of them was startled to find

From the Fourth Branch, an Ultimatum

Overlawyered.com, July 16, 1999

"The next great issue will be managed health care, said Mr. [Russ] Herman [former president of the Association of Trial Lawyers of America], whose New Orleans law firm has contributed $6 million in time and resources to the tobacco litigation with Mr. Gauthier.

"'This Congress has an opportunity to do something about it,' Mr. Herman said, 'but if they don't act, my guess is that in five years you will see a massive lawsuit brought to destroy and dismember managed care as it currently operates.'" — quoted in "Tobacco-Busting Lawyers On New Gold-Dusted Trails" by Patrick E. Tyler, New York Times, March 10, 1999.

A more recent report, by Michael D. Goldhaber in the June 28 *National Law Journal* ("Class Action Blues, New Orleans Style"), suggests that the duly elected legislative branch of the U.S. government may not have moved with sufficient alacrity to accept the terms Mr. Herman has dictated. "We're going to dismantle the managed care system," it quotes him as saying. [5.10]

that Cafe had received 10 times the amount of gold he was supposed to. The nurse had confused 50 and 500 due to metric uncertainties. Gathering a posse and racing up to the hospital room, the doctor found Cafe dressing himself in preparation to depart from the hospital. The doctors quickly put him back in bed, began administering diuretics and, as Cafe would later testify, put some serious fright in him. His hospital visit was extended. He had further tests. But ultimately he was released and, the clinic believed, had no lingering side effects from the incident.

Or so they said. Cafe believed that his health had been ruined by the episode and brought a malpractice case against the clinic seeking substantial damages, claiming every health setback in the years subsequent to the episode had been caused by that excessive injection of gold.

The facts were not the best from the point of view of the clinic. They were very sympathetic from the point of view of the plaintiff.

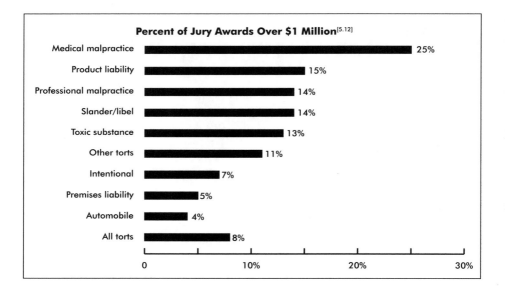

Percent of Jury Awards Over $1 Million[5.12]

Category	Percent
Medical malpractice	25%
Product liability	15%
Professional malpractice	14%
Slander/libel	14%
Toxic substance	13%
Other torts	11%
Intentional	7%
Premises liability	5%
Automobile	4%
All torts	8%

It does not take a skilled scriptwriter to lay out the plot. It is a very short story and easy to understand. "The clinic bungled. I was damaged. Make me whole."

In truth, of course, it was a no harm/no foul situation. Although frightening, the incident really could not be linked with any further health problems. The plaintiff wanted money. The clinic was willing to pay the amount of the additional hospital bill arguably caused by the incident, but no more. The plaintiff wanted a bundle.

The case would again be a battle of metaphors. The defense could choose to be defensive. We were wrong. We have no excuse. But, on the other hand, technically the patient was not really hurt that badly. Sorry.

Certainly elements of that *mea culpa* would have to be incorporated. But the "confession and avoidance" sounds flaccid. And it misses the point.

What was really going on was this: a lawyer and client were seeking to shake down the clinic for largely spurious health claims resulting from an unfortunate accident. This was, in the metaphor of the clinic, opportunism.

A thorough review of the plaintiff's history revealed certain issues relating to previous claims made to the Social Security Administration that appeared inconsistent with his current claims. His claim that he had been rendered incapable of running his restaurant business seemed to be exploded by a variety of facts. Evidence was gathered that contradicted various aspects of his story of the painful sequellae that he said attended his visit to the clinic.

What the jury was to evaluate was how and why a person would make false claims against a prestigious clinic to make for himself and his lawyer a big strike. The actual injection was moved from center stage to backstage. The real issue, one highlighted by a sharp and thorough cross-examination of the plaintiff, was the willingness of a person to say whatever it would take to create a totally false impression in court.

When the jury came back in, there was astonishment among many. We had told the jury it could award Cafe the full amount of his additional expenses from the morning of his planned departure to the morning of his actual release but should do nothing more. The jury did not even do that. It was an overwhelming defense victory in a case that, at first blush, had great danger.

The matter and the manner of the presentation joined to assign the right roles in the melodrama. The jury decided to release from the log, before it ran into the buzz saw, the good and honorable physicians and staff of the major medical clinic. It was the plaintiff who was wearing the dark hat and cloak.

The best defense is a good offense. It took courage for both the bank and the clinic to assume the uncompromising and aggressive role they did in the presentation of the defense. But such a strategy works.

The message gets around town and around the legal community that this kind of ordeal proved to be a real ordeal—for the plaintiffs. The normal mindset, that a plaintiff will either win a major victory or at least shake down defendants for a nuisance settlement that will cover their costs even in the worst case, proved wrong. Cases like these two explode that mindset.

The ordeal by melodrama becomes an ordeal for plaintiffs and counsel, indeed. Soon it becomes less popular to sue the bank or the clinic. Cases that would have been brought, are not brought. The marginal barracuda is deterred. The message is read loud and clear. Before you sue these folks, you better come in with more than metaphor, more than melodrama.

The famous Far Side cartoon has two deer standing together, one with a series of orange concentric circles over his heart. His comrade says, "that's a bummer of a birthmark."

One of the joys of defending good and honorable corporate defendants is knowing how, when, and where to apply the blaze orange paint to the adversary. And then giving the jury foreperson and colleagues the weapons to shoot at such an inviting target.

Chapter 6

The Department of Defense Plays Offense

Hell hath no fury like a bureaucrat scorned. The theology is incorrect. But the exasperation that produces such ejaculations is real.

There has long been genial speculation on why government bureaucrats can be so implacable, humorless and self-righteous. Such traits are not necessarily inevitable in the species *Enforcementus Bureaucraticus,* but they are widespread enough to create a credible stereotype.

It is the chicken and the egg controversy revisited. Do the self-righteous naturally gravitate into high-minded government service, indifferent to the seductions of filthy profit-making enterprises? Or do normal people, put into a government factory, get extruded like some piece of plastic molding into the genuine Pharisee?

Such perplexities do visit a lawyer who could have gone into either private practice or government service, but chose private practice, and thinks his character would likely be much the same in either role. For those who have been tracked down by an agency devoted to their destruction, the quality of mercy is strained to a droplet; righteous fervor reigns. The bureaucrat does his dance like a flamenco dancer angry with the floor.

If the above seems a bit over the top, ask "William Watts." William has a biography that recalls Horatio Alger.

Born in the inner city, William went to Central High School. He played quarterback on the football team, then drifted into assembly line work at a defense contractor on the outskirts of town. William, a bright and engaging African-American, did good work in electronics. But he had a dream of doing something more with his life. And with the help and support of friends he made in the business community, William decided to start his own business.

The name of the business was Spark Electronics. Its business, as its name implies, was to assemble electronic parts, largely for the defense industry. With no prior business experience, William began to assemble

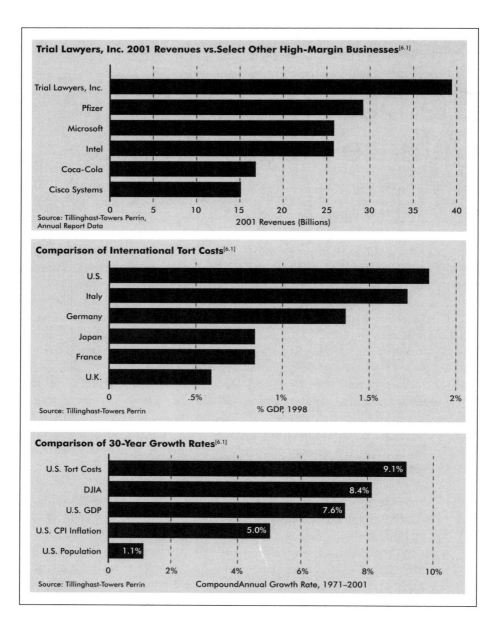

Trial Lawyers, Inc. 2001 Revenues vs.Select Other High-Margin Businesses[6.1]

Source: Tillinghast-Towers Perrin, Annual Report Data
2001 Revenues (Billions)

Comparison of International Tort Costs[6.1]

Source: Tillinghast-Towers Perrin
% GDP, 1998

Comparison of 30-Year Growth Rates[6.1]

- U.S. Tort Costs 9.1%
- DJIA 8.4%
- U.S. GDP 7.6%
- U.S. CPI Inflation 5.0%
- U.S. Population 1.1%

Source: Tillinghast-Towers Perrin
CompoundAnnual Growth Rate, 1971–2001

a team of relatives, friends and others, and using a small bit of seed capital began to build his business.

The business succeeded beyond his expectations. Both work and honors began to come his way. Spark Electronics became a subcontractor for many of the largest companies in America: McDonnell Douglas, Honeywell, North American Rockwell, and other giants in the defense industry. It put out a good product at a good price. Plaques announcing William Watts as "subcontractor of the year" and "small businessman of the year" began to grace his office. In flowed opportunities, photo-ops with President Ronald Reagan, contracts with NASA, and a host of other honors, emoluments and memberships.

While William was doing well, he was also doing good. He was a source of employment to many minorities, not only African-Americans, but Hmong and other Asian refugees. He became a friend of U.S. Senators and Congressmen. He crisscrossed the country in search of contracts. His personality and transparent honesty endeared him to business leaders and government employees. Life was good.

**Negligent misrepresentation,
Lying and equivocation,
Then give fiduciary breach a nod –
I'm drafting a complaint on fraud.**

– A young lawyer

But one day, it all changed. William got word of an invasion. Having a cup of coffee at home before heading off to work, William got the message that van loads of agents from the federal government had spilled into his corporate parking lot. They had invaded the premises, armed with side arms and other weaponry, to serve a search warrant. They began hauling off boxes of corporate records, throwing them into their vans and creating the chaos in a corporate headquarters that only execution of a federal search warrant can create.

Having no idea what this was about, William left his coffee unfinished and raced to work, finding all of the employees outside on the sidewalk or in the parking lot. There was confusion and consternation, but no answers. What was the motivation for the early morning raid?

It soon became clear. This was an investigation of Spark Electronics by the Department of Defense. It had to do with one government contract in particular. Spark had done the electronic assembly on a harness used on gun ships deployed in the Gulf War against Iraq. The product had been good, the price had been better, but the government was looking into whether it had been defrauded in connection with the price charged by Spark to the Navy.

The investigation was peculiar. The price Spark charged was more than fair, well below that of any competitor, well below that of prices paid by the government before for the same product. There was no problem with the quality of the product either. Why was the government now treating William Watts and his company like Saddam Hussein?

The risks of the dispute were obvious. When one has a contract dispute with a private party, it might end up in court. But it ends up there as a result of a civil complaint filed in a civil action. The complaint might allege breach of contract or, in aggravated circumstances, common law fraud. Every corporation has its share of such litigation disputes.

But when one contracts with the government, one risks a different kind of dispute. When the government, through one of its agencies, has a contractual dispute, it may choose to make a federal criminal case out of it. Criminalizing contractual controversies gives the government special leverage in enforcing its own interpretation of agreements.

In Spark's case, this is what led to the raid: the Spark team had worked with the government and the Small Business Administration representative to come up with an appropriate price for the electronic assembly of the harness. Such a construction of price components involves many good faith estimates, the collection of time cards of employees, the negotiation of an appropriate percentage for profit. It is a difficult art under the best of circumstances; it certainly is not a science. Even large organizations with many layers of management have difficulty.

Spark Electronics was still a small company. It had sometimes lost money as a result of estimates that did not adequately take into account the complexity or difficulty of a job. Pricing on this particular contract was one of the most difficult matters to assess in the history of the company. The company could not afford to lose money on a project of this size; it would be easy to underestimate the hours required for the job. William wanted to make sure that his team knew they should not underestimate the costs or hours involved.

After significant investment was made of time and energy, the government entities and Spark reached agreement. There would be 10 percent profit allotted to Spark. There were allocations of hours agreed for the various tasks comprehended in the contract. The price was certainly right for the government and seemed to assure a reasonable profit for Spark. Indeed, at the end of the day, whether by luck or skill in estimating, Spark made almost precisely the profit both sides agreed would be appropriate.

This was what was known in the light. But other things were going on in the dark. Two employees of the company, a father and son named Foy, were critical to the estimating process. The senior Foy had known William at the defense contractor plant. Foy had taken the young black man under his wing and given him a chance. When William had enough work to offer Foy a job, his loyalty compelled him to make the offer; Foy became William's head of manufacturing. When the elder Foy's son needed work, William was there for him as well. He added the junior Foy to the payroll.

When the senior Foy mis-estimated projects which cost the company significant losses, William forgave him. When the junior Foy had problems that should have led to his termination, William brought him back. William never forgot a friend who had given him a helping hand along the way.

What William did not know, but was soon to find out, was that the Foys, and another employee at the company, were plotting to start their own business to compete with Spark. Whether the motivation was a racist envy of William's surprising success, or pure greed, the three met secretly together, plotting their strategy, at a time when their participation in the bid process was critical. They forged a business plan. And they developed a new strategy, one designed to hurt Spark Electronics and help themselves.

They would go to the government, and turn in Spark, alleging that there had been a modification of time cards and a fudging of other data in the harness contract. In short, they would allege there had been a conspiracy within the company to defraud the government. If convincing, they could get a 10 per cent snitch bounty to fuel their fledgling business.

First impressions are key to many relationships. Once the government develops a first impression of corporate fraud, even though the person who comes in with the information ought to be viewed suspiciously, that first impression is sometimes unshakable. It was so here. The information provided triggered a major investigation. Indeed, the Spark investigation was to be designated as a number one priority of the Department of Defense that year. The DOD, the Naval Ordinance Station, and the U.S. Attorney in Louisville, Kentucky were all on the case.

When William came into my office to discuss taking the case, the disease afflicting Spark Electronics looked terminal. Even though there had been no criminal wrongdoing, the distraction and expense of a major government investigation could bring a big company to its knees, and could do much worse damage to a young and fledgling concern like Spark. Once search warrants come down, indictments are nearly inevitable. An indictment typically leads to a suspension of government contracting opportunities and ultimately, upon conviction, debarment. Government contracting was Spark's business. Any long-term debarment would be fatal.

In addition to that, of course, were the potential criminal penalties. An indictment would lead to a trial in Louisville, Kentucky where a predominantly white and rural jury panel would assess the company run by William Watts and his brother George, northern and African-American. The Federal Sentencing Guidelines for such crimes call for enormous penalties, because fraud, even in relatively small amounts per harness, can be multiplied magically into millions of dollars as a result of statutory multipliers and can lead to significant time in jail.

Notwithstanding the good character of William Watts, the unblemished reputation of his business, and the fact of his innocence, things looked dire indeed.

A trip to Louisville was not encouraging. The Assistant U.S. Attorney on the matter cheerfully announced his unbroken record of victories in federal criminal cases and clearly viewed this as a career case. Speaking with his supervisor, the head of the white-collar crime unit, and the U.S. Attorney himself, was also unhelpful. They were implacable. They wanted pleas to felonies and serious penalties. It would be capital punishment. This case would either kill the company by agreement or result in a large and costly trial that might kill the company even with a successful defense and acquittal.

There were many barracudas in these waters, and they all had very sharp teeth. But once it became clear that William's "friends" were involved, a new strategy occurred to me. It appealed to William as well. Rather than waiting for the culmination of the federal grand jury process, we sued. Not the government, but William's ex-employees. We quickly moved for documents and, as rapidly, set up depositions.

The government was outraged. And for good reason. Among the many advantages the government has in criminal prosecutions is its monopoly on the ability to discover facts through formal discovery mechanisms. The government serves search warrants, gathers evidence by grand jury subpoenas and grand jury testimony and patiently builds a case against the company—all in secret. It can methodically organize its documents, prepare its transcripts of witnesses and have a case ready for trial before the putative defendant has any access to the information the government has.

The government takes documents out of the company necessary for its trial preparation and holds them in preparation for trial while the company scrambles to put together in piecemeal fashion the documents it still has in its possession. That was true in the Spark case.

The government had all the relevant company documents that were needed by the company to put together a defense. This gross disparity in the ability to discover facts is one reason why the government can happily agree to meet the speedy trial deadlines of federal statute. The guarantee of the speedy trial right was enacted to give defendants an opportunity for prompt justice. In fact, it is often a good friend of the prosecution. While the government has its exhibit stamps already on the documents, the defendant faces inordinate complications, both factually and legally, and may be two or three years behind the curve. Then it hears a pious U.S. Attorney generously declare, in open court, a willingness to give the company its right to a speedy trial within 70 days.

Civil cases, on the other hand, are even-handed. Both sides have an opportunity to do discovery. And the civil cases launched against Spark's faithless ex-employees gave us an opportunity to even the discovery imbalance. The government, though it tried mightily, was unable to stop the litigation from proceeding. The case went ahead. Documents were discovered. Witnesses were deposed.

The results of that discovery were shocking. The ex-employees had been conspiring for quite some time. They were planning to go after Spark's customers. They gave each other assignments to head up the relationships with all of Spark's best customers. For working capital, they put in an amount they expected to receive from turning in the company. Turn in Spark to the federal government, get a 10 percent finders fee for the snitchery, and convert that 10 percent into financing for their own entity. The government would get its own pound of flesh, the new company would get a jump start, and Spark Electronics might well be out of business.

The government refused to negotiate seriously or to settle on reasonable terms. The case came on for trial in Louisville. The Number One Priority of the Department of Defense looked to have great prospects of success from the government point of view. A jury was picked with only one African-American. The witness list included the promise of adverse testimony by Spark insiders, the faithless ex-employees.

When the first of these ex-employees, the junior Foy, took the stand, the government immediately saw the dangers of a fair fight. Taken apart limb by limb, bludgeoned by documents turned over during civil discovery, Foy wanted to be anywhere else but in this courtroom during his cross-examination. The government's decision to lead off with one of the ex-employees proved to be unwise. The entire story of how the Foys sought to bite the hand that fed them, plotted against their loyal friend, and sought to use the government and its power to accomplish their own conspiratorial business objectives became the story—not the rip-off of the American taxpayer story that the government wanted to sell.

The government was thrown into disarray. Their accountant, who had worked 4,000 hours to calculate government damages for the case, came up with three different numbers over one lunchtime—each one lower than the prior—when put to sudden flight during his cross-examination. The jury laughed audibly when he was asked whether, if a further recess were taken, the government would end up owing Spark money.

As for the star witness-in-chief, the senior Foy, the catalyst and instigator of the investigation, he never appeared. Despite repeated promises that his appearance was just around the corner, the corner was never reached. The demolition job on his son apparently convinced the government that his plight on the stand would be even worse and more lethal for the government's case than the fallout from his son's testimony.

But while the case seemed to be going well, the fear and dread was palpable as the jury went out to make its decision. Had the story been convincing? The federal government wins well over 90 percent of its trials, given the inherent advantages it has in such a process. Would this be one of those 90 plus percent cases?

The pilgrimage of William Watts from inner-city kid to decorated CEO with significant management responsibilities at a much-awarded company flashed before his eyes. Through the banter and lighthearted humor of many evenings at a hotel in downtown Louisville there was a somber underlying mood. This case was not simply for the life of a company. It was for the very business life of two achieving men.

The government saw the stakes as high as well. They threw all their resources into the struggle both in Louisville and Washington. If this was to be their priority prosecution, they wanted to win.

When the jury came back, it had a resounding message. It was "not guilty" on all counts for all defendants. But there was a further message as well. As the defense team walked out of the courtroom, trailed by the prosecution, a most peculiar thing happened. The largely white, mostly rural Kentucky jury was waiting for William. Juror after juror went over to William and George Watts and hugged them. One of them said "this should not have happened to you." Another said, "I am ashamed of my government for treating a citizen like this."

As for the government, it still believed it was right. Indeed, it mounted a subsequent, although somewhat half-hearted, civil case against Spark. But that did not work either.

William Watts continued to build his company, bringing it back from its ruins, and added other lustrous chapters to his impressive résumé.

But it would not have happened if he had gone gently into that good night. He was strong enough to bite back. And but for the evidence gained by the decision aggressively to attack his attacker, he might never have prevailed, no matter how good his case.

The government, nursing its wounds with the pain only a bureaucrat can feel, was heard to grouse that the most unfair thing of the entire process was the unwillingness of a judge to shut down our lawsuit against the government's star witnesses.

There was no indication, however, that their inability to put their star informant on the stand ever suggested to the government that maybe they should not have relied on him at all in the first place.

Being a barracuda means never having to say you are sorry.

Chapter 7

Not a Class Act

It is as ritualized as a mating dance between members of an exotic species. It makes the stylized movements of the Peking Opera look positively spontaneous.

The "it" is the first meeting between opposing counsel in a class action lawsuit. On one side of the table sit counsel for the putative class. The Rolex Oyster Presidente watches are a dead giveaway. On the other side of the table sit counsel for the defendants.

Class actions were conceived to help the little guy with the little claims when a large entity oppresses a large group of "little guys." Damages to any one individual may be small, even though the damages to the group collectively may be enormous. If each individual has to sue on his own, the costs of hiring a lawyer and waging litigation against a substantial defendant would make litigation impractical. If the same individual were required to locate a large number of other individuals who have the same problem and suffered the same kind of damage before bringing suit, the individual would, of course, be at a loss. How would he go about doing so, without considerable personal expense that would dwarf any likely recovery he could anticipate?

The class action remedy seemed to be an ideal device to give small plaintiffs an opportunity to pool their claims and to get justice. The result was Rule 23 of the Federal Rules of Civil Procedure. If a group of individuals has been wronged in similar fashion, and common facts predominate, they may be melded into a plaintiff class. One plaintiff may sue and, if that plaintiff is a good representative of the entire class, and has claims typical of the class, the lawyers representing that representative plaintiff may seek to have the class certified by court. In order to give counsel the incentive to take the risks associated with a class action, the law permits class action counsel to apply for attorneys fees out of any settlement. That award will take into account not merely the time spent by the attorneys but will also include other considerations, including a "multiplier" that gives the lawyer a spiff, a potentially large fee enhancement for excellent performance, for taking significant risks, for undertaking a complex representation.

If we were to listen in on the first meeting of counsel in such an action, we would expect to find the plaintiffs' counsel in our imaginary conference room speaking boldly for his poor and fatherless clients. He is the champion of this purported class. We expect him to go to bat for the unfortunate and, with single-minded zeal, seek their benefit.

> Annual sales of legal services in the United States total more than $164 billion yearly, according to U.S. Census data. [7.2]

The opening question posed by plaintiffs' counsel, therefore, surprises us. He directs his attention not to the merits of the lawsuit, but specifically inquires as to how much insurance coverage the company and its directors have. This "D&O" coverage seems to have special fascination for the plaintiffs' counsel.

When told that there is $30 million of coverage, plaintiffs' counsel proposes a solution to the defendants' problem. Nay, he almost proposes a toast to Chubb, to AIG, and to the Saint Paul Companies.

He says, "Why don't we cut through all this early. If you guys can get us say five million dollars of attorneys' fees, you can in good faith get $1 million or so of attorneys' fees for yourself. The insurance company will likely waive the deductible. You can be a hero to your client. They will pay nothing. You get your fees. We get our fees. And it's done."

By this time, we cannot resist making our own interjection into the conversation.

"But what about the class you represent? What do they get? You are claiming, after all, that they have been defrauded, that they bought or sold stock in reliance on representations that were not true? What do they get?"

"Well," the plaintiffs' counsel says, "they get corporate therapy."

"Corporate therapy?"

"Yes, corporate therapy. We can design ways to ensure that this will never happen again. The company can appoint a director we both agree on to serve on the board. He can be, uh, an expert in finance at the local business school. That will give the class future protection against fraud. We can also design an appropriate compliance program.

Mass Tort Litigation "Exploded" in the 1980s[7.1]

	⊢ Disposed	→ Ongoing

	1960s	1970s	1980s	1990s
Beverly Hills Supper Club		200 ⊢		
Hyatt Skywalk collapse			2000 ⊢	
MGM Grand Hotel fire			1000 ⊢	
Dupont Plaza			2000 ⊢	
IMER/29	1000 ⊢			
Bendectin			1200 ⊢	
DES		1000	→	
Dalkon Shield			? ⊢	
Copper-7			1300 ⊢	
Shikey heart valve			54,000 →	
Silicone breast implants			450,000 →	
Salmonella (Chicago, Jewel Foods)			43,000 ⊢	
L-Tryptophan			4000 →	
Agent Orange			250,000 →	
Asbestos		250,000	→	
DDT (Triana, Alabama)			11,000 ⊢	
Lead			1000 →	
Tobacco (3rd wave)			? →	
HIV				1000 →
Norplant				5300 →

Source: Rand Institute for Civil Justice analyses of mass personal injury litigation, 1995–1996.

"And that is not all. There is so much more we can do. We can put in place new internal financial controls. The company can provide some additional information to shareholders. They'll feel so much better about themselves."

We are still a bit unconvinced. "All of that therapy is nice," we say, "but how about money for the shareholders in addition to money for their lawyers?"

Plaintiffs' counsel is not intimidated by the question. "Instead of money that would cut into our attorneys' fees," the plaintiffs' counsel goes on, "we can give them something even more valuable. Scrip."

"Scrip?"

"Yes, scrip. Discounts on economy-size boxes of your client's product. Two-for-one coupons to eat at restaurants. Complimentary upgrades. Ballpoint pens with the corporate logo. We can agree on some creative scrip that will cost you guys next to nothing, but that we can value at, say, $20 million or so. And, come to think of it, it will have to be worth about $20 million to justify our $5 million attorneys fee claim. That's the beauty of it all. It's win, win, and win—for everybody."

While our conference room parley may seem fanciful, the proceedings within that virtual conference room are not far from everyday reality. The first order of business is always money. And it is money for the lawyers that drives the discussion. Clients are merely ornamental.

"That's the great thing about this business," a famous class action lawyer once remarked, "I don't have any clients." Indeed, sometimes the lawyers have been the clients, as with the case of the law firm of *Greenfield and Chicles*, in which the firm's senior partner had a stable of representative plaintiffs who were really alter egos.

The "solutions" such creative counsel propose may be difficult for a board of directors to refuse. They may think the lawsuit is totally unmeritorious. Their lawyers may advise them that they have a substantial chance at winning the case. But who has the guts to chance it? What if a runaway jury visits the company with the mother of all judgments? "Tell me again," the shareholders might say, "why you didn't choose to get out of litigation without any pain, indeed without any damages at all?"

And as for the insurance company, they know protracted class action litigation will be expensive. Their lawyers will run up $5 to 10 million in bills quite quickly. And the other lawyers won't quit unless they can recoup their ever escalating costs. The moving target goes only one

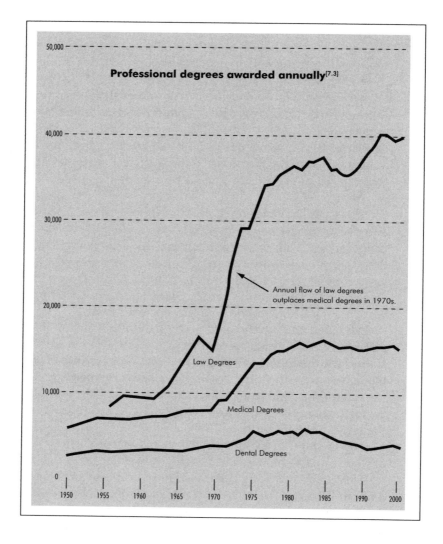

Professional degrees awarded annually[7.3]

Annual flow of law degrees
outplaces medical degrees in 1970s.

Law Degrees

Medical Degrees

Dental Degrees

way. Up. And then everyone will recommend settlement anyway. They can pay the $10 million now, or they can wait and pay the $20 million later. It is hard for the insurance company not to pay off, even though it knows that it is thereby providing high-octane fuel for the next class action soon to come.

Sensible as such solutions may appear, one thing seems to be missing from the picture: any relationship between the merits of the complaint and the ultimate outcome. Principle takes second place to pragmatism. Those who have defended class actions with any regularity are not surprised by this lack of linkage.

Whisper the word "asbestos," for example, and class-action attorneys' nerve endings begin to twitch in ecstasy. The tenuousness of the link between asbestos and injury has been documented by a myriad of studies. Nonetheless, despite this flimsy connection, trial lawyers used thousands of lawsuits to drive an entire industry to its knees while keeping for themselves a very healthy 61% of each dollar recovered.[7.10a]

We saw it again with silicone implants. Class members alleged everything from body aches to memory loss. Although ample scientific evidence vindicated Dow Corning, plaintiffs' attorneys cornered the company into a $3.2 billion settlement and drove it to bankruptcy.[7.10b] Total settlements for silicone implants: over $7 billion, with lawyers pocketing approximately one-third.[7.10c]

Class actions are not limited to widely publicized multi-billion dollar awards. Another school of barracudas alleged that Toshiba produced defective laptop computers. This unfounded assertion never even saw the light of day in court, but it was enough to make the computer manufacturer roll over and settle. In the end Toshiba was bitten to the tune of $597.5 million. Willing consumers swallowed a few mouthfuls, and the class action attorneys ate the rest. [7.10d]

But the results don't have to fall out that way.

John Stein has been a remarkably successful investor. Emerging from humble circumstances, John developed a well-deserved reputation for being one of the shrewdest investors in the United States.

THE WALL STREET JOURNAL

July 8, 2004

"Since it became the largest company in America, Wal-Mart has also emerged as the most-sued company."[7.4]

While he successfully accumulated wealth from buying and selling surplus goods, John Stein first came to prominence when he, along with Jim Smith, another wealthy investor, purchased the receivables of a company during its bankruptcy. The play initially seemed risky, especially for a conservative investor. But the brash young entrepreneur was persuasive in his effort to get some capital from the cagey investor.

He convinced his older partner that his analysis was right and the value was there.

And his analysis was right. Oh, how right. The two minted money on the deal. An informal investment yoke was formed and Smith and Stein were the yoke fellows. The two investors began a series of common investments that were almost uniformly successful.

Golf Ball Class Action

Overlawyered.com,
November 18-19, 1999

Golf Digest is "disgusted" over a class-action suit that lawyers filed against the Acushnet Company because, after running out of a promotional glove sent free to customers of Pinnacle golf balls, it sent the remaining customers a free sleeve of golf balls instead. Fraud! Deception! Shock-horror! "In the end, the plaintiffs' attorneys were awarded as much as $100,000 in fees for their heroic efforts, [Allen] Riebman and [Lawrence] Bober (as the two named plaintiffs) themselves received payments of $2,500 apiece, and everyone else received what the lawsuit claimed was unacceptable in the first place: another free sleeve of Pinnacles. That's justice at work." [7.5]

Stein became both revered and feared during the decade of the 1980s. He acquired manufacturers and a number of companies in a variety of industries. Along the way, Stein made friends of other prominent investors, appeared on distinguished panels with high-profile business leaders, and cut a stylish figure in the national business community.

Meanwhile, his colleague, Smith, had built an immense fortune, both with financial interests throughout the United States and as a result of a lucrative beverage bottling operation. The financial and bottling operations gave Smith a fortune publicly estimated at over $1 billion.

In the mid-1980s the time proved right for Stein and Smith to make another investment. After looking at a variety of businesses, the two began looking seriously at a group of stores called "Fashion."

The idea was intriguing. These stores represented the largest chain of their kind in the United States. They also had a dominant share of the department store market. Located in prestigious department stores around the country, they played on the convenience they offered their customers. Women could go shopping and, while shopping, visit these stores within stores, all in one location. They had accumulated considerable goodwill and the cachet and convenience of the department stores would be expected to rub off.

Low-Sodium Barracuda Victuals

In the early 1990's, the Federal Trade Commission claimed that Stouffer's ads falsely implied that its frozen entrées were low in sodium. Stouffer argued that the ads were truthful, but an administrative law judge disagreed and said that the ads were a "miscalculation."

Attracted by the bait, Alabama trial lawyer Randall Haynes swam into court with a class action suit against Stouffer. He claimed that his clients had been damaged by spending money on the food.

There was a minor problem with Mr. Haynes' case. It seemed that nobody could remember exactly how they had been harmed. Details were sketchy at best. Connections between the lead plaintiff and Mr. Haynes surfaced.

But that wasn't an insurmountable obstacle. The case never went to trial (the judge urged the parties to work it out), so the parties fought it out on their own. In the end, the plaintiffs got 35-cent coupons for more Lean Cusine. Haynes and company swam away with a $250,000 bite out of Stouffer. [7.6]

While the cosmetology business was one in which neither Smith nor Stein, nor the other prominent investors who would be a part of the new enterprise, had experience, it seemed to be a good story and would provide a bold new direction for them.

Stein was prepared to invest his own money in the acquisition. He also had an investment group he had put together to take over companies that, through aggressive and intelligent management, could be radically improved, enhanced in value, and ultimately realize substantial gains for investors. In the group were prominent national investors.

Besides Stein, his investment group, and Smith, there were other prominent investors who were interested, all with commendable investment credentials.

Due diligence seemed favorable. A Big Eight accounting firm was brought in. Nothing they found seemed to suggest that any representation made by the sellers about the business was untrue. Stein thought that with some cost-cutting and tough and responsible management, these entities could be managed into even greater profitability and substantial additional value could be created for the investors.

If one were a betting man, one would not want to bet against any of these investors. All were phenomenally successful. All had a great eye for value. All had good staffs, access to good due diligence, and a great track record.

Then again, perhaps they were due. The company investment in Fashion proved disastrous. The best business minds cannot ferret out fraud.

Not long after buying into the stores, the company found it had been defrauded and had to sue the sellers. The lawsuit was ultimately settled for over $10 million. But the problems continued. Strange ten-footed critters kept crawling out from under every corporate rock. News was bad, only to get worse. High-level meetings developed plans that seemed likely to stanch the hemorrhage of capital. The bleeding continued. Everyone would agree that the worst was over. It never was. Plans came and plans went. But the money drain did not stop.

As for the Humpty Dumpty at the bottom of the wall, not all the kingly investors, with their combined intellect and management smarts, could find a way to put Humpty Dumpty back together again.

The biggest losers, of course, were the insiders. It was to be the worst investment Smith or Stein had ever made.

But there were other losers as well. Many small investors, especially those represented by brokers in the local area, had taken positions in the company. Figuring that anything that Stein and the others invested in had to be good, they bought shares in the company. With Jim Smith's unbroken record of successful investment, it seemed safe. Brokers were touting the stock, largely on the strength of the prominent investors involved. Like the little fish that hitch a ride with the big fish, safely behind a fin, these felt secure. But when the big investors lost, these investors lost as well.

Ultimately the bad news came. The company was going into bankruptcy proceedings.

Following the class action convention of "suing on the news," litigation started immediately. A group of law firms began a class action against the company and its prominent investors and directors.

As with most such actions, the gist of the complaint was fraud. The big cigars had defrauded the little people. The law firms, the champions of the little guys, were now rising up to do substantial justice. They would win redress for the knowing fraud perpetrated upon the investors.

Such litigation, of the "ready, fire, aim" variety, is expected when such bad things happen to good people. It is a regular phenomenon.

Case Files:

Anchem Producs v. Windsor,
117 S.Ct 2231 (1997)

Action: Never even intending to litigate, the settling parties presented to the District Court a class action complaint, an answer, a proposed settlement agreement, and a joint motion for conditional class certification.

Background: A group of plaintiffs wishing to bring a class action suit needs court certification before proceeding. One of the most hotly debated class action procedure issues in the 1990's was whether judges should be permitted to certify classes for settlement purposes only. Rule 23 makes no provision for such classes, but certification for settlement purposes had become common by the 1990's.

Ruling: The Supreme Court ruled that certification of certain classes for settlement purposes is proper. Since over 96% of cases are settled before trial, the impact of this decision on the settlement process is obvious. Plaintiffs can now join as a class action for the sole purpose of gaining a settlement. [7.7]

But the litigation here had significant irrationality at its core. It is all well and good to speculate that big investors might sometimes willingly defraud small investors. But here the big investors lost far more than the small investors did. Indeed, Stein continued to put money into the entity at a time when the class action suit alleged he knew the company was going down the toilet. Unless he was a masochist, something not apparent from his earlier investment decisions, this would be difficult to explain. Why would sophisticated investors invest, indeed continue to invest, if they really knew there was a "cancer" eating through the body of the company?

There is, of course, no good answer to the question. I set up an early meeting on behalf of John Stein. I told the assembled lawyers for the putative class that I thought their complaint was vulnerable to motion. I told them I thought their case was irrational. I told them that they did not need Stein in the case, and indeed would be better off without us making their life miserable. I told them finally that Stein was not one they should seek to intimidate and, once efforts at

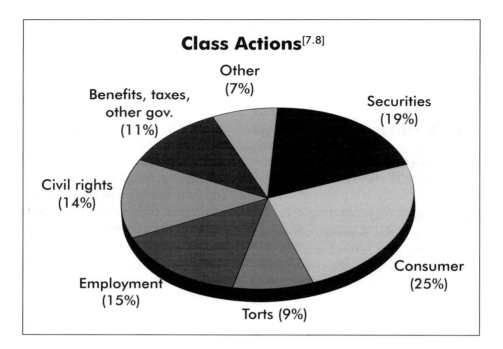

Class Actions[7.8]

Other (7%)

Benefits, taxes, other gov. (11%)

Securities (19%)

Civil rights (14%)

Employment (15%)

Torts (9%)

Consumer (25%)

peace failed, I would get instructions to try to grind them to powder. Let my people go.

After a respectful hearing they said they would get back to me. They did. They brought an amended complaint that sought to mitigate the problems with the complaint they believed I was talking about. The battle was on.

We had a nice story for a jury. It was simple and commonsensical. Our clients did not intend to deceive. They acted consistently with their words. They made an uncharacteristically unfortunate investment, notwithstanding their collective acumen. They lost. Others lost. End of story.

But we did not want to wait that long, and spend that much. We wanted to go after the plaintiffs—and quickly.

John Stein was not to be intimidated by a class action lawsuit. Knowing he was in the right, he was prepared to be resolute and unbending in these adverse winds.

Acting on his behalf, we launched a motion to dismiss. The motion alleged that plaintiffs had no evidence of scienter, no evidence that is to say that the defendants knowingly made misrepresentations. Indeed, all the evidence was the other way.

We sought to stay discovery while the court undertook a review of our very substantial motion. Why, after all, should everyone spend a lot of money for a case that might be thrown out of court? The argument made sense. It has since been given the force of law in the Private Litigation Securities Reform Act. But at the time of the litigation, the Act had not yet been passed.

The motion to stay was denied.

Over the next year, the court considered the motion. And while it did, plaintiffs' counsel went on a drunken bender of discovery. Crisscrossing the country, deposing dozens of people, taking the insiders on for multiple days of recorded testimony, the amount of pre-trial discovery was immense. Gathering tens of thousands of documents and computerizing them with the most sophisticated electronic technology, plaintiffs clearly anticipated a settlement that would constitute at least hypothetical therapy for their clients and newfound wealth for them. The lack of merit to their litigation seemed to play no role in how furiously they spent their money and time.

As one good turn deserves another, perhaps one bad investment deserves another. There were reports that the lead plaintiffs' firm had spent close to $6 million on the litigation.

Then came the shock. The judge granted nearly all of our relief and dismissed nearly all the claims. The disbelieving plaintiffs moved for reconsideration; again, the court held to the essence of its order, reminiscent of the wall plaque that says "what is there about the word no you don't understand."

Although small shreds of the case remained after the cannonball had blown apart their class action vessel at midships, the handwriting was on the wall. And it was ugly.

Among all counsel, it was estimated that some $12 million had been spent on the litigation. And there had been no trial. No one had even answered the complaint. As for the lead firm, the ultimate settlement, funded by insurance, gave them only a small fraction of their time charges, and did not even begin to cover their out-of-pocket expenses.

Showing that barracudas are more vulnerable than they might appear when first confronting the snorkeler face-to-face, this huge blood bath was one of a number of factors that caused the firm to disintegrate.

From 250 to 150 to 50 to only a memory in a matter of months. And as for Stein, he did not pay a penny. Nor did his group.

Unmoved by unmeritorious litigation, and unwilling to pay tribute, Stein shed no public tears as a last spadeful of dirt was thrown on the grave of the law firm that claimed he had committed fraud.

Chapter 8

I Don't Like You Anymore

I t has often been said a person does not know who his best friends really are. The loyal ally of today may become the implacable enemy of tomorrow. The exhilarating honeymoon may become the enervating bondage.

Relationships are not always forever. It makes no difference whether the relationships are personal, social, or business. Relationships are always more fragile than they look. That is why a cautious person, especially a cautious businessperson, understands and makes some contingency plans.

Among all the sharp-toothed barracudas swimming in corporate waters, none is so dangerous as the disaffected ex-employee. His bitterness long nourished, his enmity inveterate, he looks for opportunities for revenge, and in the current litigious climate, he frequently does not have to look very far.

If one were to investigate the most frequent catalyst for criminal prosecutions brought against legitimate businesses, one would stand out above the rest. An ex-employee has brought incriminating information to the government or to one of its agencies. If there is one witness who can turn a peccadillo into an enormous problem for a company, it is the ex-employee who turns state's evidence and testifies for the plaintiff. If there is one mother lode of negative information an

> Between 1990 and 1998, civil rights complaints in U.S. District Courts more than doubled from 18,793 filings to 42,354. About 65% of this increase was due to complaints related to employment issues, which nearly tripled from 8,413 in 1990 to 23,735 in 1998. [table/graph available][8.1]

> "[T]he the securities gravy train for Trial Lawyers, Inc. rolls on: securities class action filings rose 31 percent in 2002, and Milberg Weiss negotiated three recent settlements of $300 million or more. [tables/graphs available][8.1a]

antagonistic party will seek to mine when contending the corporation is no good, it is the disaffected ex-employee.

Because they speak as a onetime employee of the company, their credibility is enhanced, regardless of the circumstances of their departure or their personal enmities. And when they speak, their words may be taken as admissions against the corporate interest. Their interests and the corporate interest are, of course, wildly disparate. But for the judge who technically and mechanically applies the laws of evidence, the rantings of an ex-employee, or—even worse—the evil surmisings of an ex-employee, may be taken as an admission. And the jury may accept them as gospel truths.

No employee was more valued at Barbicon & Company than Ed O'Hara. O'Hara had never heard of Barbicon until he answered a blind ad in the *Wall Street Journal*. The ad sought applicants for the position of General Manager for the company's Manila facility.

Barbicon & Company was the brain child of Bob Barbicon. At the time O'Hara interviewed with the company, Barbicon was a distinguished member of Congress, representing a district in the Midwest. He was known as a fiscally conservative Democrat, and a high-minded ethical watchdog in the House of Representatives.

But the Bob Barbicon who started Barbicon & Company was a teenage boy, living in Spirit Lake, Iowa, with a fascination for fishing. That fascination led him to start tying flies in his basement. He got so good at it, that many neighbors and friends asked him to tie flies for them.

EEOC: Offbeat Beliefs May Be Protected Against Workplace Bias

"Belief in radically unconventional scientific notions, such as 'cold fusion' or cryptic messages from extraterrestrials, may merit the same workplace protections as freedom of religion, according to a ruling by the Equal Employment Opportunity Commission in a job discrimination case." The case arose from the April 1999 firing by the U.S. Patent and Trademark Office of patent examiner and astronomer Paul A. LaViolette, who claims the action was taken because he holds unconventional beliefs, including a belief in the highly controversial theory of energy generation through "cold fusion." In the words of the *Washington Post*, LaViolette's website, www.etheric.com, "details his 'proof' of the existence of alien radio communication, his theory that the zodiac is a 'time capsule message' warning of emanations from the galactic center and his views on the Sphinx, the Tarot and Atlantis, along with his considerable accomplishments in mainstream science." [8.2]

➤ An employee at a West Virginia convenience store who injured her back opening a jar of pickles was awarded $130,000 in compensation, $170,000 for emotional distress, and a whopping $2.2 million in punitive damages.[1] Since 96% of cases are settled out of court or otherwise disposed of without trial, however, actual punitive damage awards represent just the tip of the iceberg. They are dwarfed by the amounts paid out in settlements due to the *in terrorem* effect of punitive damages. In many of these cases, the threat of punitive damages may be abused as a "wild card" to force higher settlements. As Yale law professor George Priest has observed: "[T]he availability of unlimited punitive damages affects the 95% to 98% of cases that settle out of court prior to trial. It is obvious and indisputable that a punitive damages claim increases the magnitude of the ultimate settlement and, indeed, affects the entire settlement process."[2] Payments to settle lawsuits increased three-fold between 1980 and 1995, and continue to climb at roughly 7%.[8.3]

Before long, he had a little business off the ground and running. As he saw he could make money in his fly-making business, he began to work harder and longer at his basement business. The rest, as they say, is history.

Ultimately Barbicon & Company became a major manufacturer of sporting goods products. It beat major competitors in the quality of its product lines. Barbicon loved his line of work. He represented that love by making a red heart the symbol of the company.

And he had reason to love it. The company did well. It did so well, in fact, that it eventually made the decision to open a plant in Manila. Using Manila's lower manufacturing costs, Barbicon intended to import products for sale in the United States and Canada. The company learned of a tax holiday in Manila for new businesses. Combining the effect of lower costs of manufacturing and other government provided incentives, it seemed like a good way to take the company to the next level.

To do so, the company needed a competent and trustworthy manager to set up the operation. It, therefore, took out the blind ad in the *Wall Street Journal*.

Who Needs Communication?

The Equal Employment Opportunity Commission steps up its campaign of complaint-filing over employer rules requiring employees to use English on the job. Synchro-Start Products Inc. of suburban Chicago has agreed to pay $55,000 to settle one such agency complaint; native speakers of Polish and Spanish make up much of its 200-strong workforce, and the company said it adopted such a policy after the use of languages not understood by co-workers had led to miscommunication and morale problems. The EEOC, however, pursues what the *National Law Journal* terms a "presumed-guilty" approach toward employer rules of this sort, permitting narrowly drafted exceptions only when managers can muster "compelling business necessity," as on health or safety grounds. Earlier this year, a California nursing home agreed to pay $52,500 in another such case. In some early cases, employers adopted English-only policies after fielding complaints from customers who felt they were being bantered about in their presence or that non-English-speaking customers were getting preferential service—a problem which, like that of co-worker morale, may not necessarily rise in Washington's view to the level of "business necessity." [8.4]

Among the candidates, Ed O'Hara seemed to be ideally suited for such a management position. He had some training in international business, he claimed expertise in plastic, and he was an engaging person, a can-do person with an Irish gift of gab. Barbicon and the other executives liked him immediately.

There was only one dissenting voice. George Gates, the head of technology for the company, had asked O'Hara some questions to test his purported expertise in plastic. O'Hara failed miserably. Johnson was convinced that his claimed knowledge was a hoax. He warned the others to be cautious. He did not want O'Hara to be hired.

Notwithstanding Gates's cautions, the company offered O'Hara the position.

O'Hara's early history with the company seemed to validate the enthusiasm of his supporters. He got the company the tax holiday. He set up a plant with the help of a local general who had fought in World War II. And he began to manufacture rods. Periodic visits by the company president, Donald Davis, seemed to confirm that O'Hara was a man in charge, that he was truly a can-do manager. Indeed, though just a start-up operation, Barbicon Manila was quickly edging toward profitability. O'Hara was commended.

But, as the Bible says, some men prefer darkness rather than light, because their deeds are evil. If the management back home had known what was going on in the dark, it would have had a far different view of O'Hara. It would have known that George Gates's darkest surmisings were understated.

O'Hara was, in fact, totally corrupt. He was first of all a sensual man, making frequent visits to houses of ill repute in an infamous red-light resort. And he charged the company for his excesses. He put women who could not type, so to speak, on the payroll. He boasted that he was now "living out his fantasies."

"In January [1997], a former truck driver for Ryder Systems, Inc., won a $ 5.5-million jury verdict after claiming, under the ADA [Americans with Disabilities Act], that Ryder unfairly removed him from his position after he suffered an epileptic seizure, saying his health condition could be a safety hazard. During the time he was blocked from his job at Ryder, the driver was hired by another firm, had a seizure behind the wheel and crashed into a tree. Ryder is appealing the verdict." [8.5]

But O'Hara's corruption extended to matters of greed as well as matters of lust, to things big and to things small. Because O'Hara wanted to make himself rich and not simply to succeed as General Manager, he began to manufacture his own products, at corporate expense, and sell them out of the factory in Manila to the company's largest customers. With the cost of goods sold essentially zero, O'Hara would make a substantial profit on the rods. Shrewd and careful in his cover-up, he hid from the congressman, the company president and other company insiders what he was doing to feather his own nest.

But O'Hara was one of those self-indulgent few who, whatever the lack of discipline in certain areas of his life, knew how to plan ahead. Knowing that one day he might be found out, he concocted a plan.

One day, Barbicon received an urgent message from O'Hara. He would have to come to Manila. It was absolutely critical that he come personally, said O'Hara. Barbicon sought to find out what was wrong. His busy congressional schedule could not readily afford an unplanned trip halfway across the world.

O'Hara would not tell him, saying he could not talk over the phone. But he said Barbicon would have to trust his judgment and come at once. Barbicon called his lawyer, a specialist in international law. Both of them boarded the plane for Manila. When they arrived, they went to the locale where the plant was located. O'Hara met them at the train station and drove them to the small meeting room at the company.

Then he told them shocking news. In hushed tones, he confessed he had paid a bribe.

A bribe? It was unthinkable.

How could it have happened?

It was the tax holiday, O'Hara said. In order to get the tax holiday, he had been required to make a payment to a local official. He had had no choice. The life of the fledgling company depended on it.

Then came more shocking news. The second installment was due shortly. He wanted to tell them before he made the payment.

The shock turned into anger. "How could you do this? You'll have to be let go."

O'Hara began to plead for his job. Reviewing the many things he had done for the company and his sacrifices for the company, how he had moved with his wife to Manila, and how his wife and family depended on him, he pleaded that what he had done was done only for the corporate interest. He was in a difficult situation. He asked for another chance.

After some deliberation, his appeal was granted. Barbicon told him to get the money back. He said he could not. But he expressed a willingness to comply with anything else the company wanted.

After serious discussion, it was decided he did not have to ask for the money back, but he could not pay the next installment. During the course of these discussions, O'Hara told his visitors that he thought the company had customs issues that arose from his treatment of "assists."

Assists in the customs laws are an arcane concept in application though simple in principle. To figure out how much duty is owing on, for example, imported rods, one has to figure out what the value of those rods is. To do that requires constructing the costs

The longest-running mass tort in U.S. history and arguably the most unjust, asbestos litigation has so far bankrupted at least 67 companies and wrung $54 billion from helpless corporations. That's more than the total bill for all Superfund sites, Hurricane Andrew, or the World Trade Center attacks.

Estimates of the total costs of all claims exceed four times that amount—more than $200 billion. [8.6]

that went into creating the rods. Block by block, line item by line item, one constructs the total value of the import for customs purposes.

But what if value is added from the USA? What if there is assistance from R&D, or some management input, or a host of other benefits that flows to Manila from headquarters in the USA? Certain kinds of assistance, according to the Customs Service, are "assists" that need to be declared and factored into the value of the import as well. How to do the calculations, and what really is an "assist" is, of course, a somewhat scholastic question.

As O'Hara was giving his take on exposures for the company, Barbicon's counsel was taking careful notes. He was a careful lawyer who was almost obsessive in his desire to understand and record everything he heard.

The appropriate decisions were reached, O'Hara stayed and the other two headed back to the USA. When the lawyer got back to his office, he began to prepare a comprehensive trip report. He left nothing out. He wrote down facts, assertions, advice. He opined on customs issues, even though he was no expert on that arcane legal area. His lack of expertise, however, did not prevent him from reaching certain private judgments and recording them in what he assumed to be a private and privileged memo. Among these judgments was the following: "no reasonable jury," he wrote, would believe that the company had acted "in good faith." The bribery discussion was there, as well as his counsel to O'Hara that he could nonetheless give "small gifts and concessions" to the Manila official even though he could not pay the next installment of the bribe. He wrote. And wrote.

The decision to write everything down was imprudent. But his next decision was even worse. He decided to send the report out. He sent it to Bob Barbicon. And he sent it to Ed O'Hara. In doing so, he violated the "know your recipient" rule. When O'Hara's ex-wife was interviewed years later, she remembered with precise recall the day her then husband received the letter. She said Ed came home in an especially good mood that day and with a lengthy document in his hand. As she sat watching, he opened his personal safe and put the document inside.

She remembered asking why he was so happy. He replied, cheerfully, "because now I have those bastards by the (expletive deleted)."

And he had reason to believe he did. Nothing he had done had been in good faith. It is likely that he never paid the bribe. It was clear, or at least it became clear, that the company had violated no customs laws. But O'Hara had a devious mind that had hatched a devious plan. He wanted to have something on the company so when the ding dong of doom ding-donged, he would have some leverage against the company. The trip report, with all of its admissions, was just the document he needed.

Doomsday ultimately arrived. A conscience-stricken secretary in Manila mailed an invoice to the U.S. The invoice was unrelated to any business that the company had in Manila. It was, in fact, an invoice from O'Hara's side business.

The home management began to pull on the thread. What they found, after the unraveling, was amazing. O'Hara had been selling goods out the back door to the company's best customer under a different corporate name, and keeping the profits for himself.

Another delegation went to Manila, this time to terminate O'Hara. When he was confronted, he was defiant.

"You cannot terminate me. I know too much."

He threatened the company. He would turn the company in if he were terminated.

The company rejected his threats. They terminated him. His fantasy life was now finished, at least that part of his fantasy life that was financed at corporate expense.

Having nothing to lose, O'Hara went to the Customs Service of the United States government. He had quite a story to tell. Whatever his credibility might have been as a terminated ex-employee, it was enhanced—validated—by his documents. He had carefully contrived telexes to the United States that were all inlaid with connotative meaning and were full of innuendo useful for O'Hara's current purpose. And the pièce de résistance was, of course, the trip report.

After a period of silent gestation, a new and major customs fraud examination investigation burst forth. In a lightning commando style raid in the city of the company headquarters, a flotilla of government vans full of armed government agents stormed the otherwise peaceful headquarters of Barbicon & Company. With apparently indiscriminate interest, tens of thousands of documents disappeared into bankers' boxes, which then disappeared into vans, to be hauled to customs headquarters. The search warrant was based on an affidavit. And the affidavit, sealed from view, was based on the testimony of one Ed O'Hara. What O'Hara told the agents, however objectively fishy, had apparently been uncritically received and believed. The government took the bait—hook, line and sinker.

The agents were not interested in finding out details of O'Hara's sordid past. Nor were they interested in hearing nuances about the law of assists. The documents were clear to them. O'Hara's testimony was clear to them. Since the company was owned by a Congressman, this would be a career case for agent John Gotham and for Assistant U.S. Attorney David Luxemburg, with help from the customs service in Washington, D.C.

Indictments followed. It would be a nightmare for anyone, especially for a politician known for his ethical commitment and strong religious core. This was an indictment that could kill his company and kill his career. Even though the Congressman was not indicted himself, other associates were. Indicted with the company was the president, Don Davis, the chief financial officer, Raphael Peller, and a secretary/customs clerk, Sally Diamond.

There are three phases of white collar crime representation. First, one tries to avoid indictment. Second, one tries to avoid trial. Third, one tries to avoid conviction.

Pursuing the first objective leads one to try every aspect of moral persuasion possible, including seeking a review at the Department of Justice. That was done. The government was obdurate.

The second objective is implemented in legal motion practice. Here, the government had engaged in dirty pool. The search warrant had been improperly obtained and executed. The government's view of the law was unprecedented. The indictment was defective. Such irregularities rarely move a court. They did not move the court here, except on behalf of Diamond and Peller, peripheral defendants. They were dismissed. That left the last resort: win it at trial.

After all the skirmishes and motions, the case would, for the remaining defendants, ultimately go to trial. All the strategy and tactics, deployed pretrial, must be designed not to interfere with any chance of winning it before a jury at trial. O'Hara, the Barbicon barracuda, would not get his pound of flesh, or his 10 percent spiff, without a fight. The company would go to war.

Again, the company position, at our suggestion, was relentlessly aggressive. We sued Ed O'Hara while the criminal matter was pending, eliciting cries of outrage from the government. We had a good case against him. And we needed to know what he was saying to the government. We did not want to hear his side for the first time from the witness stand of the criminal trial. He was a loquacious and savvy man, untrammeled by truthfulness or a conscience. Cross-examination, without discovery, would therefore be a challenge. In the civil case we could take his deposition.

Through several days of deposition testimony, Mr. O'Hara, believed by us to be a pathological liar, had to explain his behavior over several years of questionable activities. With questions coming at him from strange angles, not knowing always what was in his best interest, O'Hara's testimony was a crazy quilt of information and self-contradiction, generating testimony difficult for him both to remember and later to reconcile. And difficult for an experienced cross-examiner not to love.

The point of the civil litigation, of course, was not to get Mr. O'Hara's money. By this time, he had none. Or if he had some, he was smart enough to make sure we would never find it.

But the gold mine we were digging in was the gold mine of information, finding nuggets to be used in the inevitable litigation, United States vs. Barbicon & Co. And gold it was. Inconsistencies, contradictions, white lies and whoppers.

There would be difficult things for us to explain to a jury, not least the assertion in the trip report that no reasonable jury could believe that our customs decisions were in good faith. But if those difficulties had been aggravated by allowing Mr. O'Hara to testify against us without having any ammunition to use against him, the trial would be nearly hopeless.

The value of such an aggressive posture became clear on the eve of trial when the judge granted our request for a hearing on our motions to exclude evidence prior to trial. At the hearing, we were allowed to cross-examine O'Hara before the jury was selected.

At this point, we had a choice to make. Should we cross-examine O'Hara in a limited way, holding back our best cross-examination material to surprise with before the jury? Or should we go after O'Hara, seek to rattle him, to destroy his credibility with the Judge and eliminate some of his testimony?

Believing barracudas are meant to be bit back, I lunged at O'Hara during cross-examination. Over more than two hours of cross-examination prior to trial, I sought to hound him from pillar to post, pulling factual cudgels derived from discovery in the civil case out of transcripts and beating him around the head with them. Again and again, O'Hara was impeached. He lost his confident air. He had the look of a fighter examining the canvas for the best place to fall.

By the end of the cross-examination, O'Hara was exhausted. Since he calibrated his answers by what would be in his personal best interest, questions that were disguised left him uncertain of which way to jump. Again and again, he felt the stinging rebuke of facts. He was a proud man, unused to taking verbal beatings. The strain and fatigue of the ordeal showed. By noon that day he looked like a beaten man.

The impression was not lost on the Judge. Obviously troubled by what he had heard, the Judge took a recess. Then he invited the U.S. Attorney into chambers for an ex parte chat. We never heard what was said. But the gist of what was said was clear.

The Judge had been so troubled after hearing the cross-examination of O'Hara that he had told the US Attorney that O'Hara could not testify. The government, in a two-hour hearing, had lost their star witness, their insider, their disaffected ex-employee.

The Judge during the trial would refer to Mr. O'Hara as a "known perjurer." He even referred to him as such in jury instructions he later read to the jury.

The trial lasted 11 weeks. But our decision to sue O'Hara civilly, with the fruits of pre-trial discovery and intense preparation now fully ripened, was paying off. The government case, highly publicized and high-profile, was crumbling. We suggested in mid-trial that the government reconsider the case in the light of the evidence and do the right thing. The government should dismiss the case.

During a recess in the midst of the trial we met in Washington with representatives of each of the four or five government agencies involved in the case, all with their own government acronyms and GS-ratings. Though the government knew it was in trouble, no one was willing to bite the bullet. The first hour of the meeting was spent determining whether the government had the authority to dismiss the case and if so which agency had that authority and if so which specific regulation allowed it. It was a bureaucratic jungle of people trying to protect their turf and defend their backsides in no particular order of importance and not make a decision they might be criticized for later. Their long-cultivated skill in not making decisions showed. We went back to trial.

Notwithstanding the difficulties presented by the documents, not least the trip report, the defense was strong. We thought we should win. We knew we ought to win.

As we sat in the Kellogg Apartments across the street from the court-house, the defense team waited in our "war room" for the phone call announcing that a verdict had been reached. With me was my colleague Brian Palmer and Tim Barbicon, Bob Barbicon's son, a Stanford graduate who had mastered the case and who would ultimately become the CEO who would oversee the company's emergence as the dominant company in its product lines in the world.

We joked. We discussed sports. Seeking distraction, Barbicon buried his face in a *Wall Street Journal.*

Then the phone rang. Only then did I know the pressure Tim was under. As the phone rang, Tim split the *Wall Street Journal* perfectly down the middle, unintentionally. We answered the phone. The jury had returned.

The longest time in any trial is the time between the return of the jury to the courtroom and the reading of the verdict. The foreperson, eyes deflected, gives the verdict form to the marshal. The marshal gives it to the clerk. The clerk hands it up to the judge. The judge silently reads it without betraying his feelings or the result it contains.

The judge gives the document back to the clerk. The clerk reads it. The caption and jurisdictional headings take an eternity. "The United States District Court…" he drones on.

Finally, he gets to the important part. "Not guilty" on each of the first two counts read individually. Then, mercifully, the clerk having reviewed the verdict says "counts 3 through 41—not guilty." The president of the company is acquitted as well. It is a total victory.

The U.S. Attorney led the government team out of the room, mumbling to an officer of the Customs Service, "well at least you learned something about civics."

We raced over to call Congressman Barbicon, who immediately had a press conference announcing the good news. He and his company had been completely vindicated.

A good and decent man, he was grateful and showed it. He was later to tell a group of airline passengers when we happened to be sitting near each other on a flight back from Washington, "this man saved my life." A nearby passenger asked my wife in a stage whisper, "is your husband a doctor?"

As for the government, their warriors still did not give up. They attributed the result to only one cause: we had won the case because of the reasonable doubt standard. They wanted another chance on a civil standard.

They still believed O'Hara. Their lack of flexibility was yet another example of the law of first impression. When someone drops suspicious circumstances in a prosecutor's lap, he tends to believe the worst. No factual reproof will later change his mind. He will blame cunning lawyers, and try and try again.

Round two was as unsatisfying for the government as round one. The government is not always a quick study.

But important lessons can be learned by potential targets. Beware of people who expose even small chinks in their moral armor before you hire them. When someone admits to doing something seriously wrong, fire him and never look back. Beware of the disaffected ex-employee. They, like Mac the Knife, have a sharp and concealed blade they would like to insert deeply into the corporate body that hurt their feelings when it fired him.

Barbicon & Company would survive—and thrive. But no thanks to Ed O'Hara.

I got a call years later from the company. The caller, a corporate officer with Barbicon & Company, had a question. "I have something of some interest for you, counselor," he said. "We just got a job application in response to a blind ad we placed in the *Wall Street Journal*."

"So how can I help you with that?" I asked.

"Well, we thought you might be able to help us review the credentials of this particular candidate."

Confused, I asked how I could possibly help do that.

"We just wondered if you knew him," the caller said.

"His name is Ed O'Hara."

Chapter 9

Caveat Vendor

"Litigation is edging closer and closer to extortion every day." [9.1]

Most lawyers, given the trauma, dilemmas, and occupational frustrations of practice, have had the thought come to mind: law would be so much easier to practice if only one did not have clients.

The Biblical proverb puts it another way. "An empty stall is clean but there is much gain by the strength of an ox."

The same is true of the mind set of any businessperson who has known the ox droppings left by a disaffected customer. Sometimes it is the residue of buyer's remorse. The customer, dazzled by the warm and radiant light of the showroom bathing the new automobile, and his animal spirits excited by the new car fragrance, agrees to buy a shiny new vehicle redolent of Corinthian letter. Then he goes home to explain the purchase to his wife. Before long, he's claiming the car is a lemon, and he seeks to have it returned and his money refunded. Buyer's remorse.

Or it may be the smoker who cannot get enough nicotine. Contentedly puffing away at what he jokingly refers to as his cancer sticks, he finds some euphoric fulfillment in sucking that sweet smoke into his lungs. Years later, however, he sees no irony when

An airliner was having engine trouble, and the pilot instructed the cabin crew to have the passengers take their seats and get prepared for an emergency landing.

A few minutes later, the pilot asked the flight attendants if everyone was buckled in and ready.

"All set back here, Captain," came the reply, "except one lawyer who is still going around passing out business cards." [9.2]

✳ ✳ ✳

"Everybody in my family follows the medical profession," said John. "They're all lawyers." [9.2]

Some plaintiffs succeed in turning everyday events like spilled coffee into multi-million dollar verdicts. In 1992, Stella Liebeck spilled a cup of coffee on herself as she held it between her knees in a car. The theory? McDonald's made hot coffee, so it was liable for her burns. The jury smacked McDonald's with a $2.9 million verdict. [9.3]

lawyers and state attorneys general working on his behalf (and in the interests of the taxpayer) are collecting billions of dollars on the strength of the peculiar argument that the true risks of these "coffin nails" were unknown to him. $360.5 billion later, tobacco companies realize the dangers of having customers.

No matter the product, one can always find a lawyer to make trouble. The search is easier when the lawyer has his own website. A customer's lawyer may be only a click away at www.greedylawyers.com. As a web site with that name makes clear:

> In a country filled with laws and lawyers, you need to pick the one that is best for you. You need a greedy lawyer who has the best chance of winning your case with persuasion, devotion, intelligence, and with productive presence.

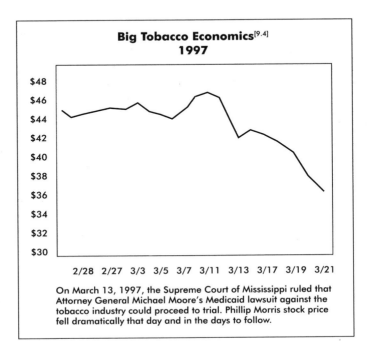

Big Tobacco Economics[9.4]
1997

On March 13, 1997, the Supreme Court of Mississippi ruled that Attorney General Michael Moore's Medicaid lawsuit against the tobacco industry could proceed to trial. Phillip Morris stock price fell dramatically that day and in the days to follow.

Louise Crawley's lawyers won a class-action suit against DaimlerChrysler after she sustained minor burns from gases released when an air bag deployed in an accident, although she conceded the air bag saved her life and protected her pregnancy.

In addition to awarding her $730 in actual damages and $3.75 million in punitive damages in February 1999, the jury ordered an estimated $63.89 million to cover others in the class.

"The verdict just defies common sense," says Jay Cooney, spokesman for Chrysler's legal team. "The plaintiff walks away with burns that go away a week later, and the company gets hit with $60 million. It's bizarre." [9.6]

Why would you want a greedy lawyer? We think the question should be "why would you not want a greedy lawyer?" The lawyers at greedylawyers.com are forceful and determined to help and not leave you empty-handed or in debt. That is why greedylawyers.com is the place for you! Our lawyers have what it takes to get you your money. Our lawyers are proud to be greedy; they are greedy for their clients; greedy for you!

The "greedy" lawyers of the ad, however, quickly become the "gallant" lawyers for the little guy when they enter the courtroom. Controversies with customers, after all, always have a David and Goliath feel. When it comes to a large company and a small customer, only one side will have the jury of his peers. No one has ever seen a jury of 6 or 12 corporations. But juries will always have 6 or 12 customers. In a medical malpractice case, there will be no doctors on the jury. But the jury will, on the other hand, be composed of nothing but patients. Every juror will have had an unacceptable commercial transaction in the past. Far fewer will have had an unfortunate experience with a customer. And if they have, there will almost always be sufficient peremptory strikes for the plaintiff's lawyer to take care to remove him.

BMW sold a new car without disclosing a touch-up paint job, which arguably reduced its value by $4,000. This refinishing policy was legal in most states. An Alabama jury decided to punish BMW by multiplying $4,000 by the 1,000 refinished cars that BMW sold nationwide, arriving at a $4 million verdict for a single Alabama plaintiff. [9.7]

Asbestos-Related Bankruptcies, 2000–2002[9.5]

A-Best

AC&S

A. P. Green Industries

Armstrong World Industries

ARTRA (Synkoloid)

Babcock & Wilcox

Bethlehem Steel

Burns & Roe Industries

Eastco Industrial Safety Corp.

E.J. Bartells

Federal Mogul Corp.

G–I Holdings

Harbison-Walker

J. T. Thorpe

Kaiser Aluminum and Chemical

MacArthur Companies

North American Refractory Co.

Owens Corning Fiberglass

Pittsburgh Corning

Plibrico

Porter Hayden

Shook & Fletcher

Skinner Engine Company

Swan Transportation Corp.

USG Corporation

Washington Group International

W.R. Grace

Source: American Academy of Actuaries

The normal result is therefore that the vendor is on the defensive against the purchaser. It is the typical paradox. While the old bromide says "caveat emptor," the reality is sometimes "caveat vendor." While we know that the borrower is often servant to the lender, it is not infrequent that the lender becomes servant to the borrower, especially if the debt is large enough.

It is often wise to settle up with customers before the issue is formally joined in a court of law. It makes sense for many reasons: to avoid the worst outcome; to remember that business considerations must sometimes be paramount regardless of the merits of the case; to avoid any unnecessary expense of litigation; to minimize the distraction of employees and executives, and other tangible and intangible costs of litigation.

There are times, however, when it makes sense to fight. And when fighting, there are few and limited occasions when it makes sense to use the Muhammed Ali Rope-a-dope. Muhammed used the strategy during his celebrated "rumble in the jungle" with George Foreman but it was not his typical approach. A more generalized strategy was comprehended in his slogan, " float like a butterfly and sting like a bee."

When I was a young partner, the senior securities litigator in the firm came into my office and plopped a file on my desk. It was called Durocher vs. Dain, Kalman and Quail. Dain was a long-time client of our firm. It was a stock brokerage with a substantial presence throughout

Suing Like Crazy

Reader's Digest, October 2000
Trevor Armbrister

"There's cash in out-of-court settlements, but the biggest money comes out of cases that go to trial. In Lowndes County, for instance, Alex Hardy and his wife sued General Motors after an accident left him paralyzed. Hardy's Chevy Blazer had left the highway and rolled over, throwing him from the truck. GM argued that Hardy admitted to having a few beers; the plaintiff argued that his blood-alcohol level was zero after the accident.

"Trial lawyer Jere Beasley said GM was at fault; the theory was that the Blazer's rear axle had fractured, causing the accident. In addition, Beasley and his colleagues said the latch had failed to hold the door closed during rollover.

"Defense counsel worried about the objectivity of Lowndes County Judge A. Ted Bozerman. Beasley's firm had represented Bozeman's wife in a lawsuit until about a week before the Hardy trial was scheduled to begin. GM's lawyers asked him to recuse himself. Bozeman refused. The state Judicial Inquiry Commission backed him up.

"Then a paralegal working for the defense said she heard a juror ask, 'How long are we going to have to sit here and listen to these lies?' GM's lawyers asked the judge to interview her to see if she'd already made up her mind.

"Bozeman refused, saying no other juror heard her remark. The jury held GM liable to pay the Hardys $150 million, including $100 million in punitive damages. After GM filed an appeal that cited, among other grounds, the judge's failure to interview the juror, Beasley and his team accepted a settlement, details of which are sealed." [9.8]

the western half of the United States. It had a number of offices in the state of Montana. One of them was in Great Falls.

The Great Falls office had a customer named Robert Durocher. He had actively traded securities through one of Dain's brokers. Not all the transactions were profitable. The result was somewhat painful for Mr. Durocher, who had a margin account with Dain. A series of margin calls left him without enough resources to cover his margin debt. His account was closed out, with a balance owing.

Ness Motley's aide-Grégoire.

Overlawyered.com - November 17, 1999

In a single day, December 8, 1999, Christine Grégoire, the attorney general from the state of Washington who's been mentioned as a possible AG in a Gore administration, saw her re-election campaign kitty more than double. The benefactors, who sent nearly $23,000, weren't Washington residents at all, but rather two dozen lawyers and their relatives associated with the Charleston, S.C. law firm of Ness, Motley, which is expected to pocket a billion dollars or more in fees from the multistate tobacco settlement that Grégoire was instrumental in brokering. An aide to Grégoire, who engaged Ness Motley to represent Washington along with the many other states it represented, dismisses talk of payoffs and calls the contributions "a reflection that someone has a high regard for an elected official." "I only wish we had given her more," says Ness superlawyer Joe Rice, quoted in this article in Mother Jones spotlighting the sluicing of tobacco-fee money to friendly Democratic pols. [9.9]

The Dain broker pointed out that he had interviewed Mr. Durocher when he opened his account. He had determined his objectives. He had fulfilled the requirements of the "know your customer" rule.

It was also true that the customer had made the final decision on each one of the trades in question. While the broker had sometimes made recommendations, he had made no "discretionary" trades in the account. He was no mere order taker. But he did not control the account in any meaningful sense.

None of these facts, however, stopped Durocher and his lawyer from suing Dain. He alleged violations of section 10(b) and rule 10b-5 of the Securities Exchange Act of 1934. He claimed the broker had made material misstatements and omissions in connection with the purchase or sale of securities. His was not the case of a person who guessed wrong on the stock market and lost. His was a case, he alleged, of securities fraud.

My partner had tried the case before a jury of Durocher's peers. The result had been a victory for the plaintiff and against Dain. One might say, it was also a victory against the evidence. My partner now was asking me (as an example of how, in large firms, work flows downhill) if I would handle the appeal.

Summer 1999, California:
Biggest Non-Class-Action Products Liability Award Yet

On the night of December 24, 1993, a 1979 Chevrolet Malibu, driven by Patricia Anderson, stopped at a Los Angeles traffic light when it was struck from behind by drunk driver, Daniel Mareno. Experts estimate that Mareno was traveling at least 70 mph. Mareno's impact crushed the Malibu's rear and pierced the fuel tank. Patricia Anderson, her children, and an adult passenger all survived. However, all occupants suffered burn injuries—from mild to severe—after gasoline leaked from the Malibu's ruptured fuel tank and caught fire.

On July 9, 1999, a California jury returned a $4.9 billion product-liability judgment against General Motors for the accident - the largest personal injury verdict in the nation's history. The award was later reduced to a still unprecedented $1.2 billion by the California judge who had presided over the trial.

The case is a study in how mismanagement of the evidence process can contribute to an outrageous verdict. . . .

Jurors found defendant General Motors 95 percent responsible - and the driver who caused the crash only 5 percent responsible - for the tragic accident. On July 9, 1999, the jury returned a $4.9 billion verdict against GM, $107 million in compensatory damages, and $4.8 billion in punitive damages. On August 26, the trial judge reduced the punitive award to a still-record $1.1 billion. . . .

Here's what the jury wasn't allowed to hear before it returned its $4.9 billion judgment:

The driver who struck Patricia Anderson's vehicle, at over 70 miles per hour, was legally drunk, with a blood alcohol level 2.5 times the legal limit in California, even hours after the incident. Moreno was so drunk, in fact, that he was unable to remember the accident;

The Chevy Malibu amassed a superb safety record for 20 years and millions of real-life miles;

That more than 98 percent of all cars built during the 1970s had the fuel tank in the same location as the Malibu;

Testimony about fuel-tank crash tests showing the safety of the Malibu design, and the problems with the alternative design suggested by the plaintiffs' lawyers. . . [9.10]

Appeals from jury verdicts are always an uphill battle. Appellate courts are usually looking for the exit sign that allows them to avoid difficult decisions. When juries have heard the evidence, the appellate courts are more than willing to overlook "harmless errors" and are reluctant to substitute their judgment for a jury's even when it appears in retrospect overwhelmingly against the evidence.

Taking over this case was, however, something of a command performance. And for a young lawyer it had a significant incentive. Expectations were low and, therefore, the rewards of an unanticipated success were high. I took the case.

> A jury in Galveston, Texas, ordered Honda of America to pay $48.75 million to the parents and estate of Karen Norman, a pediatric nurse who drowned when she accidentally backed down a 17-degree boat ramp and couldn't unbuckle her seat belt. Honda had argued that the woman limited her own dexterity because she was legally drunk (her blood-alcohol level was 0.17 percent). [9.11]

> Although million-dollar payoffs occur most often in medical-malpractice cases, product liability cases consistently are the most costly. According to the *Washington Times*, the median award against a manufacturer is $260,000. [9.12]

The legal arguments underlying the appeal might be intriguing for a lawyer but are not terribly material here. Suffice it to say, we won a respectful hearing. We also, to my surprise, won the appeal. The result was a dismissal of the case with leave for Durocher to re-file the case in federal court and try again.

Once the order came down, and the celebrations were over, it was time to wait for Durocher to file again in hopes that he would not. Or was it time to wait? Was there an alternative for us to wait patiently for our unhappy customer to take patient aim and then fire at us again?

In talking with our client, I noted that Durocher owed us money on his margin account. That had been the basis of our counterclaim, rejected by the jury in the first trial. I also noted that our broker had testified that Durocher had other accounts in Great Falls before coming to us. In following up on these accounts, I found that he had left margin balances at two other brokerage firms.

It was hardly an epiphany. But it was an "aha" experience. Perhaps we could sue Durocher before he sued us.

If he is inclined to use section 10(b) and Rule 10b-5, why should we not use the same theory? He who lives by the sword, dies by the sword. All we needed to recover was to prove a material misrepresentation or

How Do You Fit 12 People in a 1983 Honda?

Brazen, well-organized car-crash fraud rings thrive in the Big Apple, according to a series of *New York Post* exposés this summer. Other states are well ahead of New York in enacting legislation aimed at curbing fraud; meanwhile, the "Pataki administration is in court trying to overturn a decision in which the trial lawyers and medical profession successfully sued to have the state's existing no-fault regulations thrown out." June 25 (related story); June 26; June 27; July 16 (related story); August 6). Last year New York City recouped $1 million following the racketeering and fraud convictions of attorney Morris Eisen, a one-time major filer of injury claims who prosecutors say introduced fraudulent evidence in at least 18 cases, including three against the city. [9.13]

omission in connection with the purchase or sale of stock. There was such a material misrepresentation here.

We could argue that Durocher had purchased stock through our brokerage firm while making a material omission. The material omission was what he did not tell us. He did not tell us that he would not pay for the stock if it declined in value. He was using us as a guarantor of his investments. If he made money, he would keep the proceeds. If he lost money from his somewhat risky trading activity, he would not pay his bill. He had only an upside.

This, we alleged, was fraud.

We sued. Wrong-footed, Durocher had no choice but to assert his claims as a counterclaim. Notwithstanding his protestations at being the defendant, the bemused federal judge thought our action appropriate and allowed the alignment of the parties—Dain as plaintiff, Durocher as defendant—to continue.

The result was more than an altered caption of the case. It was an altered context of the case. Now we were suing a deadbeat. He was seeking to avoid paying his debt by making a number of fatuous claims of securities fraud. He was now defending himself. Before, he was the one taking the initiative, accusing us of fraud. We were compounding our alleged fraud by insisting he pay off the debt created by our broker's fraud — some chutzpah.

But now the chutzpah was his. Before they ever heard Durocher's side of the case, the jury heard ours. They heard a pattern of leaving unpaid bills with other brokers. They heard our sympathetic broker

Breakthrough for plaintiffs on latex gloves?

A Calif. jury returned an $800,000 award to a health care worker against Baxter Health Care, which formerly made latex gloves for hospital use. Naturally occurring substances in the gloves sometimes trigger virulent allergies in health care workers which prevent them from continuing in medical work, and lawyers have argued that had Baxter instituted a practice of washing the gloves before sale to remove surface proteins, it would have reduced their allergy-stimulating potential. Hundreds more latex allergy lawsuits are pending, and lawyers are hoping the new case, McGinnis v. Baxter Health Care, will serve as a model for others.[9.14]

give his side of the story. He testified that he had no idea that Durocher would not pay his bills. He had no idea that Durocher would not live up to his obligations. Durocher had never told him that he only intended to pay for his stock if it went up in value.

By the time Durocher came to the stand, the jury was looking at him with crinkled eyes. They were suspicious. Their arms were folded.

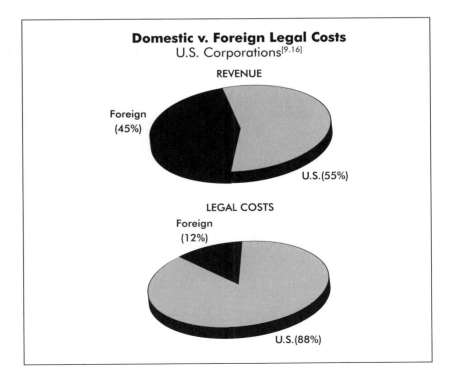

Domestic v. Foreign Legal Costs
U.S. Corporations[9.16]

REVENUE

Foreign (45%)

U.S. (55%)

LEGAL COSTS

Foreign (12%)

U.S. (88%)

Tobacco: Why Stop at Net Worth?

July 10, 2000 – Trial judge Robert Kaye, presiding over the Engle tobacco class action in Miami has declared that in calculating a basis for punitive damages there's no reason jurors should feel obliged to stop at a sum representing the tobacco companies' net worth. "There's much more to this case than net worth or stockholder equity," he said. Earlier, Judge Kaye ruled that it was proper to place before the jury the companies' capacity to borrow funds to help meet a punitive damage award, and also agreed to let the jury consider companies' operations worldwide in assessing those damages, though foreign countries might wonder why the hypothesized victimization of smokers worldwide should result in a punitive payoff exclusively to (certain) Floridians, and though overseas court systems are generally far more averse than ours to the award of punitive damages. Moreover, Judge Kaye "barred the defendants from arguing to the jury that they have already been punished enough by their earlier settlements with states valued at $246 billion" even though those settlements took place in the shadow of demands for punitive damages. (Imagine copping to a plea bargain in one court over your past doings, and then finding you get no double jeopardy protection when hauled up for punishment by a second court—after all, your plea bargain was "consensual," so how can it count as punishment? But American courts are in fact permitted to assess punitive damages against civil defendants an unlimited number of times to chastise them for a single course of conduct, so it's not as if any due process is owed or anything.)

Plaintiffs offered an expert witness, Prof. George Mundstock of Univ. of Miami School of Law, who testified that the nation's five biggest cigarette makers "are worth $157 billion domestically and have a 'strikingly rosy' future," per AP, which appears to make hash of suggestions that lawyers' efforts previous to this point have made a vital difference in putting us on the road to a "smoke-free society." Mundstock's methodology reportedly reduced to a present value stream the surplus of all future tobacco company income over expenses. Even the *Wall Street Journal*'s Milo Geyelin, not a reporter suspected of pro-business leanings, writes that Kaye's handling of the legal issues in the suit has been "unorthodox." At the *New York Times*, meanwhile, reporter Rick Bragg last month interviewed several of the dozen or more smoking-ravaged spectators who throughout the trial have taken highly visible seats in the courtroom day after day where the jury can hear and see their labored breathing, oxygen tanks, and mechanical voice boxes. While extracting considerable human-interest content from these interviewees, Bragg's story does not display the least curiosity as to whether the idea of attending just happened to occur to all of them spontaneously, or instead, as defendants have hinted, was the result of an orchestrated effort by plaintiff's attorneys Stanley and Susan Rosenblatt, which might have been ruled out of bounds as manipulative and prejudicial by a jurist less agreeable to the plaintiffs' cause than Judge Kaye. [9.17]

They were good citizens who paid their bills and showed little sympathy with someone who did not.

We won the case. The jury gave us everything we asked for. They found that Durocher had committed securities fraud.

They also took little time in disposing of his unmeritorious counterclaim. And the verdicts withstood appeal.

I good-naturedly went back to the legendary litigator who had given me the file. I dropped the judgment on his desk and told him, "You know it would be easier if you just gave me these the first time." Fortunately, that chutzpah went unpunished.

But the result underscores the point. The two trials had almost exactly the same evidence. They had exactly the same parties. They had essentially the same jury. It was a trial of exactly the same issues. No rabbits were pulled out of any hats.

But what had changed was significant. The biter and the bitee.

Chapter 10

When It's Hot, It's Hot

My client, headquartered in the western part of United States, had always considered itself a good corporate citizen. It had not had one legal blemish, much less one public relations black-eye, in its distinguished history.

Starting out as a trader of hides and furs about the time Lewis and Clark had completed their adventures, the company had in later years developed a variety of other businesses as well. Among them were landfill sites and other waste disposal facilities.

In running these facilities, the company had always taken care to abide by environmental regulations. They were not midnight dumpers. Notwithstanding the risks inherent in any such operation, as environmental sensitivity grew, the company felt sure that no one would find any intentional wrongdoing in these businesses.

Then came the helicopters. And the vans. And the government agents in gas masks and spacesuits. Right behind them came the press.

Before one could say EPA, the company's site in Pocatello, Idaho was overrun with these Martian-like invaders. Combing the dump for capacitors, other electronic paraphernalia, and any telltale signs of PCB contamination. A small army of agents did their work while others in the corps installed a command and control site. They also set up a public relations location in a double-wide trailer driven onto corporate property. Media had been alerted to

> The longest known jury trial in American history involved claims that the plaintiffs were physically injured by a dioxin spill. The jurors awarded the plaintiffs only $1 in actual damages, which reflected their understanding from the scientific evidence presented that the dioxin spill had not caused personal injury to any of the plaintiffs. Nevertheless, the jurors proceeded to award $16 million in punitive damages.[10.1]

> "[T]he Environmental Protection Agency estimates that cleaning up all 1,210 sites on the Superfund National Priorities List will cost $36.3 billion." [10.3]

the raid. Soon the somber-faced federal agents were describing for television audiences how the local water supply may have been contaminated as a result of environmental crimes committed by the company.

Surrounding neighbors were interviewed. Tearfully, fearfully, simple people cried on camera at the thought of what carcinogens might be racing through the bloodstreams of their children. People unburdened themselves of anxieties about what health problems they and their children might have as a result of the seeping of hazardous chemicals into the aquifer. The television stations milked the drama and the trauma for all it was worth.

For the company, it was a public relations nightmare. It was also the beginning of a hugely expensive and intrusive government investigation. Why had this occurred?

The answer was not in the alignment of the stars but in the alignment of political forces that often determine where this kind of barracuda will attack next.

The 1980s marked the first decade of a new era of white-collar crime enforcement. Criminalizing business activities had been a hit-and-miss proposition. Classical legal learning had always taken the view that corporations could not commit crimes. The famous legal commentator, Blackstone, said "corporations cannot commit crimes because they are fictitious persons." Presumably, fictitious persons can only commit fictitious crimes.

Burford, the English law lord, put it more colorfully. "Corporations cannot commit crimes, because corporations have no conscience. They have no soul to be damned or body to be kicked."

The theory began to be tested with the passage of the Sherman Antitrust Act prior to the turn of the twentieth century. The authors of the legislation put in criminal provisions for willful violation of the antitrust laws. The wave of social adventuring called the New Deal brought in a series of regulatory provisions, creating new regulatory agencies and new regulatory infractions. Most of these laws included criminal enforcement provisions.

Despite the criminal laws lurking in the otherwise unremarkable bureaucratic statutes, little was done to enforce them in any systematic way. Typical criminal defendants remained the same. Gangsters in

Judge rebukes EPA enforcement tactics.

August 2, 2000

"In a harsh rebuke to the federal Environmental Protection Agency's pursuit of criminal polluters, a judge has ruled the government unnecessarily harassed a Northbridge mill owner and pursued a case against him even though it didn't have any credible evidence." Following up on a tip from a former employee of the mill, which makes wire mesh used for lobster traps, a "virtual 'SWAT team' consisting of 21 EPA law enforcement officers and agents, many of whom were armed, stormed the [mill] facility to conduct pH samplings. They vigorously interrogated and videotaped employees, causing them great distress," wrote federal judge Nathaniel Gorton. Moreover, EPA in obtaining a search warrant apparently concealed evidence from its own testing indicating that the plant's wastewater emissions may not have breached federal standards. "The case marks the first time in the region that a judge has ruled in favor of an application of the Hyde Amendment, a three-year-old federal law that allows an exonerated defendant to seek legal fees from the government if the criminal prosecution was 'frivolous, in bad faith or vexatious.'" [10.3]

double-breasted suits hiding behind their floppy lapels, with sharkskin lawyers/mouthpieces at their side, coming out of grand jury rooms having "taken the Fifth."

Even into the early 1980s, whole industries had never seriously been touched by any sort of criminal enforcement. But something paradoxical was about to happen.

During the Reagan revolution, a new era of more limited government was being launched. Taxes were lowered. A variety of regulations were eliminated. Civil and administrative regulation of business diminished, at least at the margin.

But at the same time that administrative restrictions were being lightened, criminal enforcement was being increased. And such enforcement was triggered by a new and effective catalyst: political coincidence.

When the Grace Commission examined the defense industry in the early 1980s, it found widespread abuses in government contracts. They became the stuff of stories journalists are ready to die for. One thousand dollar toilet seats; five hundred dollar hammers. The worst suspicions of the populace about major defense contractors appeared confirmed.

Up to the time of the Grace Commission, no major defense contractor had ever been indicted. Within two years, five major defense contractors had been indicted. Within five years, a majority of the large defense contractors had been indicted. Years later, virtually none had escaped a serious criminal investigation or criminal prosecution.

One prosecutor draws blood, and the other sharks pay attention. It is said that when a single bee finds honey, rather than gorge himself, he selflessly goes to his friends and brings them back for a sweet feeding frenzy. So do the busy bees of white-collar crime enforcement.

The problems of my client were not the problems of the defense industry. But they were analogous. In the middle of the Reagan Administration, the head of the EPA, Anne Gorsuch Burford, got herself into trouble. There were Congressional hearings. An atmosphere of scandal hung over the EPA. With typical partisan piling on, Mrs. Burford became increasingly embattled. The result was inevitable. She had to resign. Anne Gorsuch Burford would become a footnote of failure in the Reagan Administration.

The Law is the true embodiment
Of everything that's excellent.
It has no kind of fault or flaw,
And I, my Lords, embody the Law.[10.4]

—The Lord Chancellor in "Iolanthe"

Politics being what it is, it was important for the Administration to show toughness. A new broom sweeps clean, as they say. A new EPA administrator was appointed. He vowed to get tough on environmental crimes. Get tough he did.

EPA agents were called in from all over the country and told to fan out to all the nation's regions in full environmental hue and cry. But it was not simply EPA agents who were so instructed. Agents from the Fish and Wildlife Service, Customs agency and other government departments were all brought into the struggle for a clean environment. For all one knows, homeless people were brought in from their shelters, deputized, and told to find hazardous wastes under the nation's bridges.

Within a year of the new broom sweeping the countryside clean in the restless search for dirt, 47 new environmental investigations were initiated. With such a broad-based assault, it was to be expected that not all the investigations were of equal quality. But quality is in the eye of the beholder. Accusations have their own inherent force. And when

Leave That Mildew Alone

It's illegal to market "mildew-proof" paint for bathrooms and damp basements unless you go through the (extremely expensive) process of registering the paint as a pesticide, claims the federal Environmental Protection Agency, which is seeking $82,500 in penalties from William Zinsser & Co., Inc., a Somerset, N.J.-based paint manufacturer. [10.5]

they relate to matters as sensitive as health, cancer, and the environment, they will always be taken seriously.

The allegations against my client certainly were.

EPA allegations were uncritically accepted by the media and by the TV and radio outlets in Idaho. The prefixes "cancer-causing PCBs" were used thousands of times. Every story repeated the same two paragraphs of how the investigation commenced and which cancer-causing substances were likely to have seeped into the water supply.

Indictments would soon follow. They constituted a wide-ranging set of charges against the company and certain of its executives. It also constituted a kind of regional catharsis. The wrongdoers had been apprehended. They were going to stand trial.

As we prepared for trial, however, we found serious problems with the government investigation. The rush to judgment triggered by political realities was evident. Corners were cut. Evil surmisings trumped good prosecutorial judgment. Documents that might have been exonerating had been withheld. Government bullying replaced the principal prosecutorial obligation to "seek justice, not convictions."

We, of course, attacked back. We attacked and attacked. But our serious charges never became the story. They were largely ignored. The government story was shorter and more compelling. A long and difficult trial followed. Under the intense scrutiny of cross-examination, government allegations began to melt away. Felonies disappeared like ignis fatuus over a swamp in the morning light.

"Regulation is out, litigation is in. The era of big government may be over, but the era of regulation through litigation has just begun."[10.6]

By the time the trial was ended, the only convictions were lowly misdemeanors. We appealed even these to the Ninth Circuit Court of Appeals. Then Judge (later, Mr. Justice) Anthony Kennedy wrote an opinion dismissing

Environmental Sweetheart Suits

Rarely does a month go by that the Environmental Protection Agency (EPA) is not sued by a big environmental group, often in an attempt to force the agency to crack down harder on its regulatory targets. Naturally, the public assumes that the agency and its litigious opponents are genuinely at odds over some issue, but nothing could be further from the truth. In reality, EPA often wants to be sued by environmentalists and agency records indeed reveal that it hands out millions of taxpayer dollars to the very organizations that routinely take it to court.

The relationship between greens inside and outside the government is having an adverse effect on environmental policy.

Massive environmental statutes like the Clean Air Act and Clean Water Act give EPA numerous strict mandates and nearly impossible deadlines in which to meet them.

Further, many of these laws empower environmental groups to petition EPA to go even further. When EPA fails to perform one of its delegated tasks or act on a petition, these groups can sue in federal court, forcing the agency to do so.

In this way, activists set the nation's environmental agenda to an extent few outside Washington realize. Far-reaching policy decisions are made by "public interest" environmental lawyers, based entirely upon their litigation choices.

Such legal actions have been branded sweetheart suits because they frequently benefit EPA and are tacitly encouraged by the agency. In fact, every time EPA "loses" one of these cases, the result is an expansion of the agency's power and authority. The process also provides EPA with a degree of political cover when enacting costly or unpopular measures, as it can always say that it was required to do so by a court of law. The already-dubious adversarial nature of these proceedings is further undercut by the fact that the very same litigants are supported generously with EPA dollars.

Environmental Protection Agency records show that most major environmental groups are simultaneously on the dole from, and in the courthouse against, the agency.

Six organizations have racked up at least five grants and five lawsuits in the past decade, including the Environmental Defense Fund (EDF), American Lung Association (ALA), and the National Wildlife Federation (NWF) at a cost of $36.3 billion. [10.7]

The Vast Tort Lawyer Conspiracy?

Tort Lawyers' Secret Weapon

WHAT THE AIEG DOES
The Attorneys' Information Exchange Group is a central warehouse storing internal corporate documents uncovered in product-liability litigation, among other things. Based in Birmingham, AL, the nonprofit group is an arm of the American Trial Lawyers Assn. in Washington and has a staff of nine.

HISTORY
Founded in 1980, the AIEG began as an informal network of plaintiffs' attorneys with Ford Pinto cases. Fed up with the carmaker's hardball litigation tactics, they began sharing internal corporate documents and trading tactical tips. Since then, its scope has grown. It now has specialized units for everything about autos, from tires to airbags. Other groups are devoted to school buses, motorcycles, and boats.

SECRECY
The AIEG doesn't want corporate defendants to know what documents are in its databases. So the group has an elaborate set of rules to ensure that the contents of its library remain secret and protected by attorney-client privilege. Members of the group are forbidden from disclosing what paperwork the AIEG possesses. Nor are the documents posted online. Plaintiffs' attorneys usually have to travel to Birmingham to see them.

COST
Last year, the AIEG's 600 members paid a $1,000 initiation fee, plus annual dues of $500. [10.8]

the remaining misdemeanors. The client had been 100 percent vindicated. At least in the eyes of the law.

The Pocatello television outlets were still unconvinced. In its final mention of the story, after hundreds of other mentions in prior weeks and months, a station gave its own epitaph to the story. The journalist covering the investigation gave the Ninth Circuit result, and before sending back to the news anchor said, "and so, Fred, it looks like the company has gotten off scot-free."

The company had not gotten off scot-free. It simply had been found not guilty. The expense of the investigation and trial, to say nothing of the dogged and determined government civil proceeding, would exhaust company treasuries and company executives before full vindication was achieved both civilly and criminally.

But there is a moral to this story as well. Beware the Ides of March. When the political worm turns, there is more than one Brutus or Cassius who will hatch plans to take advantage.

First comes the report of a problem: troubles in the defense industry; scandal in the EPA; a finding that some bank has laundered money; problems with major agricultural companies in their sale of goods under a government guarantee program to foreign countries; or savings and loan executive suites with original paintings and rosewood desks. And before you know it, the government lurches into action.

They increase their cops on the beat and charge them to sit under viaducts in their speed traps. They give them ticket books full of citations and tell them to find crime and reach their quota. Unsurprisingly, indictments begin popping up like popcorn. Until 1985, the "Big Bank" always thought of itself as a victim of crime. Soon it is surprised to find one of its own, the Bank of Boston, indicted. Then it finds another of its brethren, Bank of New England, indicted a year later. Within four years, 1001 financial institutions had been indicted. Then the Congress of the United States enacts three new statutes in four years enhancing penalties for "banking kingpins," treating financial institutions as mercifully as drug cartels. Big Bank had better take notice.

None of these prosecutorial trends is, of course, without some foundation. But once the government is incited by such political mischief, its discretion is tested and often found wanting.

In such cases, as parachutes drop from government airplanes and the media specialists arrive from Washington, there is no alternative except to fight. And there is no substitute for victory.

Chapter 11

Florida 2000

"Hello, Roger. This is Daniel Webster calling from Florida. I have some questions for you, and I wonder if you could give me a call back."

So began a voice-mail message and, with it, a venture into one of the two or three most important political cases in the history of our nation. It was the evening of the Thanksgiving holiday, 2000.

I, like millions of other fascinated citizens, had been following the presidential election and its contentious aftermath. But I was following from afar, with an interest in the outcome but no participation in the proves. Then came the telephone call.

When it arrived, my cell phone was off. I was in a semi-comatose state, not far enough removed from dinner at the Thanksgiving table to think clearly. My corporeal energies were allocated to digesting a motherlode of turkey, dark and white meat, and, not least, Swedish lingenberries spread generously over rice pudding. As I relaxed in my favorite leather chair, I was the poster child for "post-prandial fatigue."

Experts in cross examination sometimes advise trial lawyers to save their best questions for the hour immediately after lunch. The strategy apparently is that with the "PPF" factor—a product of the body being too distracted by digesting food to think—the locus of focus goes from the mind to the stomach, and the witness cannot think clearly enough to handle rapid-fire questions from an experienced cross examiner.

PPF or no PPF, the "CPB" factor (cell phone bondage) was stronger. I had eased the cell phone out of my pocket and found I had one message at 9:00 p.m.

I was more than prepared to wait until Friday, or even Monday, to return the call. But when I mentioned the call to my more politically astute son, Peter, he gave me some good advice. "Papa, if it's from Florida, I think I would return it tonight."

Daniel Webster, a descendant of *the* Daniel Webster, had been the first Republican Speaker of the Florida House of Representatives. Because of term limits, he was now in the Florida Senate. He was among an inner-core of Republican leaders in the Florida Legislature. He had some questions about legal and political strategies in the light of the on-going controversy between the Bush and Gore campaigns in Florida. At the conclusion of a brief Thursday evening phone call, he mentioned he would get back to me.

The next morning the president of the Florida Senate, John McKay, called me. He wanted to hire me to represent the interests of the Florida State Senate in matters relating to the election. He had the power to do so, interestingly enough, because the Democrats had a few years earlier given the president of the Senate the unilateral authority to hire lawyers to represent its interests without a vote of its members and, for that matter, without consultation of the minority. I accepted the engagement.

I was immediately cast into a reticular and fascinating legal thicket. Because such controversies happen only every century or so, there was no form book for a trial lawyer to follow. Because the questions were in part chastely constitutional questions, and no law firm has among its litigation, real estate, tax, corporate, and estate planning departments, any department called the "constitutional law department" there was no group with special expertise to consult or to deploy. In such circumstances, if a litigator does not have intuition, it shows.

The challenge for the Florida Senate, and the legislature as a whole, was threefold. The first challenge arose out of an unprecedented litigiousness about the result of the Florida presidential election vote. The margin, as we all know, was millimeter thin. Recounts and challenges in such circumstances were expected. But no one anticipated the extent of the litigation that would follow. By the time I was retained as lead counsel for the Florida Senate, 41 separate actions had been filed throughout the state of Florida. Hundreds of lawyers, like locusts, had descended on Florida. Hotels and motels bulged with the ingestion of so many out-of-state professionals. No one from the legislature had anticipated the Braobdinagian Invasion.

But what was to be the reaction? The legislature had, after all, been assigned a critical role to play by the United States Constitution in presidential elections. But how was it to act out that role as the drama unfolded?

The challenge of framing an appropriate response to the controversy was heightened by the second issue. The legislature had a difficult, somewhat distrustful, relationship with the Florida courts, especially the Supreme Court of the state of Florida. The Florida Supreme Court has a reputation as one of the most activist, if not *the* most activist, state Supreme Court in the nation. The legislature had seen that Court rule a number of its newly enacted statutes unconstitutional with almost casual ease, on grounds that often seemed shaky at best, pure judicial imperialism at worst. It sometimes appeared to the legislature that the Florida Supreme Court conceived of itself as a Super Legislature, a third political chamber that was happy to write into law its own public policy inclinations.

> ➤ The U.S. Supreme Court handles about 10,000 cases every year.
>
> ➤ Of the Court's 10,000 annual cases, only about 100 are selected for review and oral argument. [11.1]

Given those legislative perceptions, leaders in the Florida legislature had no confidence that the plethora of litigation now working its way through the courts would get a principled determination by the Supreme Court.

Those fears seemed confirmed when, days earlier, the Supreme Court appeared to rewrite Florida election law in *Bush v. Palm Beach County.* There the Court had decided that the Florida Constitution allowed it to interpret "discretion" to mean "no discretion," "shall" to mean "shall not" and "may" to mean "must." Should the legislature, which had not been involved in the case because it had not yet been officially constituted acquiesce in such a judicial amendment of laws it had created?

The third challenge was in an arena political leaders are more familiar with—the arena of public opinion. Even as early as Thanksgiving time, Democrats in particular were suggesting that there were plans afoot in the Legislature to "hijack the election." It was thought that they would seek to "steal" the election and "frustrate the will of the people." Effective metaphors frequently imprison debate. Those who have been out-metaphored find it a struggle to make their positions known, and particularly difficult to make them persuasive. The hijacking theme had seemed to be effective. Polls indicated that fewer than 10% of the American public thought the Florida legislature should intervene in the controversy at all. Could the Legislature act in the face of adverse public opinion in this complicated and controversial arena?

A final challenge was to select a prudent course among a plethora of conflicting strategic directions. There were voices in the Bush campaign that wanted no interference in the litigation that was working its way up to the Supreme Court. There were political voices within the state of Florida suggesting that, whatever were the legislature's responsibilities under Article Two of the United States Constitution, it would be political suicide to intervene and name a slate of electors. The conservative course would be to sit this one out entirely and to allow the courts to decide rather than the legislature. There were problems with both cautionary voices. If the legislature had both the right and the responsibility to frame the election laws, why should it not seek to have its voice heard when those laws were re-interpreted or misapplied in the courts? And if the United States Constitution gave the legislature, not state government generally, and surely not the judiciary, the final responsibility to select electors, why was that not the highest of responsibilities for a state legislature? And why should not the legislature make sure that a slate of electors was sent to Congress, representing the 6.5 million voters of Florida, in a way that assured Florida's voters would not be disenfranchised as a result of the uncertainties coming from the multiple litigations around the state of Florida?

Given such challenges, the Florida legislature could easily have played the ostrich. It could have hunkered down and sought to weather the storm. Instead, after a great deal of soul searching and legal and constitutional reflection, the Florida legislature decided that it had no choice but to have its voice heard. It decided to go forward with an aggressive strategy in each of the three arenas.

On the Friday I was retained, I immediately began to gather a team to work on an amicus petition for certiorari before the United States Supreme court. With leadership in place for both the Florida House of Representatives and the Florida Senate, the legislature could now take a position before the United States Supreme Court. The Supreme Court would be invited to reverse *Bush v. Palm Beach County*. That Court nominally applying the Florida Constitution, essentially re-wrote critical provisions of Florida election law. Although saying it was engaging in conventional, garden variety judicial interpretations of conflicting statutes, the Court made some curious "interpretations" that seemed more like ad hoc judicial legislation. Does "shall" mean "shall not." Does "the discretion" of Florida's Secretary of State, Katherine Harris mean she really had "no discretion?" And, of course, can "may" mean "must?" We would do an amicus petition for certiorari.

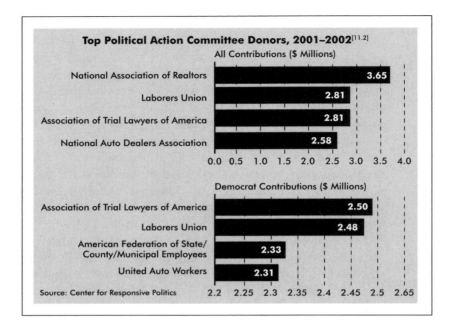

Getting the Supreme Court to intervene looked dubious. The trick was to find a way to get a federal question before the Supreme Court that would constitute a persuasive invitation to the Supreme Court to intervene. The petition drafted by lawyers for the Bush campaign was well-written, of course, but unlikely to succeed. Their emphasis was on Section 5 of Title 3 of the federal election law. In implementing the constitutional theme—Article I, Section 2 of the United States Constitution—the legislature selects the method of choosing electors in presidential elections and Congress counts the votes of those electors to determine the President. In this scheme, Congress had created a "safe harbor" for legislatures, a way to assure them that their electoral votes would be counted. Assuming that the legislature had selected the method of popular election to choose their presidential elections, there was a way the legislature could be assured the electors so selected would be able to cast their votes for President without challenge in January. The way had conditions. By the first Wednesday after the second Monday of December it has to be clear that the election had been conducted by rules in place and unchanged at the time of the popular vote. In that case, there was a "safe harbor" and the legislature could be assured that congress would count the votes of that state. Here the retroactive modifications of election law done by the Florida Supreme Court suggested that the election and any resulting certification had not taken place by laws already in effect at the time of the November 7 election. This changing of the rules midstream was the centerpiece of efforts by the Bush campaign to get the United States Supreme Court to intervene.

A problem with that theory, of course, was that Section 5 provided merely a "safe harbor." It did not affirmatively compel the states to do anything as a matter of federal law. And it surely did not prohibit them from doing anything as a matter of federal law. It merely said that if you did things in the way that Congress set out, the state could be assured of a safe harbor. I was somewhat doubtful about the chances to get certiorari.

My pessimism proved unjustified when—in the middle of drafting our petition—the Supreme Court announced that it would hear the case. Now the door to review was wide open. Our amicus, supporting the petition for certiorari, became an amicus brief "in support of neither party" in an existing case to be argued before the United States Supreme Court.

The Florida House had selected one of my former professors, the distinguished constitutional scholar, Charles Fried, of the Harvard Law School, to represent them before the Supreme Court. I was chosen lead counsel for the Florida Senate. Between our offices, we generated a brief that we thought had a distinctive voice in the controversy, the voice of the legislature. It cited a case that neither party had cited before the Florida Supreme court, a cast know as *MacPherson*.

The *MacPherson* case arose out of a controversy in the state of Michigan in 1892. The state legislature there had decided that a state election for President should not be a winner-take-all bonanza. Instead, each congressional district would have its own elector selected by the voters of that congressional district. A

"That beast"

Initially, all attorneys wore formal "morning clothes" when appearing before the Court. Senator George Wharton Pepper of Pennsylvania often told friends of the incident he provoked when, as a young lawyer in the 1890's, he arrived to argue a case in "street clothes." Justice Horace Gray was overheard whispering to a colleague, "Who is that beast who dares to come in here with a grey coat?" The young attorney was refused admission until he borrowed a "morning coat." Today, the tradition of formal dress is followed only by Department of Justice and other government lawyers, who serve as advocates for the United States Government. [11.3]

2% victory by one candidate in Michigan would not give that candidate all the votes of the entire state. Each congressional district would have its own determination as to which elector should be designated for which slate as a result of the votes in that particular district.

In assessing this innovative state system, the Supreme Court in *MacPherson* could not have been stronger in suggesting that the state legislature has a "plenary" and absolute power to determine the method of selecting electors. It even suggested, in a dictum that became important to this litigation, that having given the power to popular election, the legislature could take it back at any time. In other words, a state legislature could select electors without having a presidential election. If it chose to have a presidential election, it could take back the power to select its own electors "at any time." This case, ignored by both camps to this point of the litigation, became a centerpiece of our amicus brief.

> The publication of a Supreme Court term's written opinions — including concurring opinions, dissenting opinions, and orders — approaches 5,000 pages.

> Some opinions are revised a dozen or more times before they are announced. [11.4]

There was one other important provision in the *MacPherson* decision. It held that there was such a plenary power present in the state legislature that not even the state constitution could be allowed to stand in the way of the legislature exercising its prerogatives. Was there lurking in this particular holding, an important federal question that might allow the U.S. Supreme Court to intervene in the election controversy? Had not the Supreme Court of Florida allowed the constitution of the state to interfere with the legislative provisions enacted by a sovereign state legislature using its powers under Article Two of the U.S. Constitution?

Over the next three weeks there would be three important briefs to file on behalf of the Florida legislature. The first was the brief in *Bush v. Palm Beach County* before the U.S. Supreme Court. The second was a brief before the Florida Supreme Court on remand in that case. The third was the final U.S. Supreme Court hearing on the subject, *Bush v. Gore*. Each was due at a peculiar time, on short notice, requiring total eclipses of normal weekend activities. A great electronic triangle between Minneapolis, Minnesota, Cambridge, Massachusetts and Tallahassee, Florida came alive with multiple drafts,

The 2000 Court

> **Chief Justice William H. Rehnquist** (born 1924, appointed from Arizona in 1972, and elevated to Chief Justice 1986).

> **Justice John Paul Stevens** (born 1920, appointed from Illinois in 1975).

> **Justice Sandra Day O'Connor** (born 1930, appointed from Arizona in 1981).

> **Justice Antonin Scalia** (born 1936, appointed from Virginia in 1986).

> **Justice Anthony Kennedy** (born 1936, appointed from California in 1988).

> **Justice David Souter** (born 1939, appointed from New Hampshire in 1990).

> **Justice Clarence Thomas** (born 1948, appointed from Georgia in 1991).

> **Justice Ruth Bader Ginsburg** (born 1933, appointed from New York in 1993).

> **Justice Stephen Breyer** (born 1938, appointed from Massachusetts in 1994). [11.5]

sent and revised at all hours, before the final product was ready for inspection by the Court.

But none of the hearings before the judiciary, not even the very last one, matched the drama of the first U.S. Supreme Court hearing in *Bush v. Palm Beach County*. People began to line up outside the Supreme Court building at 8:00 p.m. on the evening prior to the argument for an opportunity to squeeze into the public galleries. By the time of the argument the next morning, the line was several blocks long and only the lucky few were to get even a taste, five or ten minutes, of the argument itself.

Even more impressive was the line of lawyers which began to form about the same time on the other side of the Supreme Court building. Lawyers admitted to the United States Supreme Court bar are given special seating when arguments occur. They are taken, on a first-come-first-serve basis, to sit behind the lawyers litigating the case. But seldom do lawyers arrive at the Court more than an hour early for such a privilege, even to hear interesting cases. Here a long line formed of those willing to spend an entire night on the cold sidewalks of Washington, D.C. to attend this argument.

When the courtroom began to fill, one could look around and see many notables. Senators and Congressman took their places. Renowned journalists took their seats, notepads in hand. Ted Kennedy, Orrin Hatch, George Will and others sat with palpable anticipation. The Who's Who of Washington political life were present. And retired Justices made their presence known. Justice White, looking frail but alert, took a seat in front of what otherwise would pass for jury box, sitting sideways to the Court. Lawyers at counsel table made notes to each other, and gave greetings to opposing counsel, the oral advocates stared vacantly, trying to put together the last elements of arguments that had been polished, re-polished, vetted, and mooted out during long preparation sessions. Ted Olson, a savvy appellate lawyer, often associated with Republican issues, was to be the chief protagonist for the Bush team. Professor Lawrence Tribe, a Harvard constitutional law scholar, was to argue the case for the Gore team. With cameo appearances from a lawyer representing Secretary of State Harris, the cast of oral argument was complete. It was decided by us, representing the Florida legislature, that we would not ask for oral argument for a variety of tactical and strategic reasons, even though it would have been likely that argument would have been granted. The case came before celebrity.

The clerk of court pounded on the gavel, and the Court filed in. As the presentation by Ted Olson began, my fears about the lack of a federal question seemed to be well-founded. The first eight questions, fired at Olson by five different Justices, all had the same tenor. "Where is the federal question her, Mr. Olson?" They seized on Tribe's argument, contained in the appellee's brief, that the safe harbor provision was just that, a safe harbor. It did not give any special federal jurisdiction. One could wonder why the Justices had granted a hearing to this case if they did not think there was a federal question when they reviewed the petition. But I had thought Tribe's position was likely to be sustained on that basis and had been surprised by the granting of cert. Now things looked bleak, indeed, for any substantive ruling.

The tide did not begin to turn until midway through Professor Tribe's argument. Then Justice Scalia began a more fruitful line of inquiry. Did not the Supreme Court of Florida, he wanted to know, really overturn or revise election laws of the Florida legislature on the basis of the Florida Constitution? Tribe gently dodged the question, knowing its potential seriousness. Scalia pressed on. Did not the Court use the Florida Constitution as a cudgel to cuff up the work of the Florida Legislature? he said in so many words. Justice Breyer intervened to suggest that the references to the Florida Constitution were more generic and genteel. But Scalia would not be deterred. If in fact the Florida Constitution was used to alter the work of the Florida Legislature, was that not a problem under the *MacPherson* case? He wanted to know.

The influence of our amicus brief seemed to be taking hold. The argument seemed to be appealing to a number of the more conservative Justices, as reflected by their questions. Soon Tribe's time was almost up and there was room for only one more question, this one by Justice Ginsburg, whose prior questions had all looked as though they could have been framed by the Gore team. Knowing the reports that the Florida legislature was preparing to anoint its own electors to an election, would it not be unconstitutional for them to take back the power and appoint electors?

At this point, I was most curious about Tribe's response. Professor Fried and I had talked about the curious way Gore's reply brief had handled our argument. It seemed to both of us that Tribe agreed with us and worded his brief in such a way that the agreement was not obvious. We both had chortled that we had at least convinced Tribe of our argument.

What would Tribe say now? He paused for what seemed like an eternity, but what was in fact probably ten seconds. He responded, in effect, that he had looked at that question in some detail, but he simply did not know the answer to it.

That response was so telling that I was able to take it back to the Florida legislature and comfort those who were straddling the fence on whether the legislature could appoint its own slate of electors. It was now obvious that it could. If the chief counsel for Vice President Gore could not come up with an argument against it, surely there was no good argument against it. I had argued that this confirmed that the legislature could appoint electors if this matter were not resolved by the middle of December.

When the result came down, it appeared that the Court was sending the case back to the Florida Supreme Court to get it right. It appeared also that the liberal members of the Court may have joined in, figuring the Florida Supreme Court would simply modify its rationale with the same result, allowing a recount that might change the results of the election. But our arguments had had an impact. And their weight became clear when, at the next argument before the Florida Supreme Court, the Chief Justice of the Florida Supreme Court had demanded at the very outset of the argument to know why neither party had brought to the Supreme Court's attention the *MacPherson* case, which seemed to be the most significant case of them all for purposes of deciding this complicated issue.

The rest, as they say, is history. The Florida Supreme Court, now bitterly divided, adjusted the time of the election again, and refused the invitation of the U.S. Supreme Court to get it right. The case bounced up to the U.S. Supreme Court again. And with the clock ticking on various statutory deadlines, the U.S. Supreme Court was able to cobble together a bare majority. That majority, in a somewhat murky opinion, hung its hat on an admission made by David Boies at the hearing below, and adopted in the holding of the Florida Supreme Court in *Bush v. Gore*. it was a finding that the Florida legislature had the discretion to determine that the state should take advantage of the safe harbor provision.

Given the fact that the Legislature had that discretion, and the period for entering that safe harbor was now over and no recount could somehow pilot the results into that safe harbor, the Court found that "school was out" and no recount was possible. Justices Scalia, Rehnquist and Thomas gave a more clear explanation in their concurring opinion based on our argument in *MacPherson*. But even in the majority opinion there was an interesting paragraph. The Court cited *MacPherson* for the proposition that not even a state constitution can stand in the way of a Legislature's sovereign right to determine the method of selection of electors. And the Court said, again quoting *MacPherson,* that once having yielded the power to the electorate, the legislature could take back the power "at any time." The double-barreled holding of the majority made clear that the Gore team had been defeated. Even if it could find a way back through the legal thicket to have another recount, the legislature had been told that it had the power to appoint electors. The arguments of the legislature had prevailed in court.

The second ring of combat was in the legislature itself. The final result before the U.S. Supreme Court could not have been foretold. It was therefore important to have electors in place who could vote on December 20, 2000, so that the slate could be sent to Congress and counted. Some outside the Legislature had proposed that the Legislature just wait until the last minute and, as a *deus ex machina*, swoop in and appoint electors to save the day and make sure the electorate was not disenfranchised. Such a process would have been unfair and politically inept. If that effort was to appear to be just, there had to be a deliberate process to explain the legislative role and to seek to give it legitimacy. We decided to have a slow and deliberative process. A "select committee" of leading Republicans and Democrats from the Florida House and Senate had hearings. I was both the lawyer for the legislature and an expert before the panel. I helped prepare other constitutional experts and made suggestions about who might be leading experts with diverse points of view. The hearings were televised. Arguments were made on the issue of whether the legislature could appoint electors and when it would be necessary to do so.

I spent hours before the Select Committee, and later before both the House and the Senate individually, explaining the interaction of the U.S. Constitution and the Florida election law. Behind the scenes, Jim Langdon, a partner of mine, and I talked to staff members about timing and wording. We drafted a resolution appointing electors. We had an office immediately outside the Senate chambers and were there from morning until night, handling staff questions, meeting with House and Senate leadership, and answering questions from the media. A ring of satellite trucks surrounded the Capitol. The sound trucks would gulp their daily ration of gasoline from a gasoline truck that would make the rounds and with ecumenical fairness would fill up all the network and cable channel vehicles that were parked around the building. Excitement was in the air, but there was serious work to do.

The ultimate schedule called for the House to take up the matter of appointing electors the day before December 12, 2000. The Senate would take up the matter the next day. I had periodic meetings with groups of legislators, answering their many questions. Were they going out on a limb, as a legal matter? Would enacting this slate of resolutions, after the safe harbor date but before the electors had to meet, be adequate? What was the *MacPherson* case all about? What was the Supreme Court likely to do? Through all these questions, I became increasingly impressed with the seriousness of the senators and representatives I met. They clearly wanted to do the right thing, and they wanted to do it in the right way.

The day before the Supreme Court was to decide in *Bush v. Gore*, the House had appointed its own slate of electors. It was the same slate that would have been selected had the initial intervention of the Florida Supreme Court not occurred. I had talked to every Republican member of the Florida Senate chamber. It was clear that we had the votes. If there was any questions about the result of the election after the Supreme court ruling, or if the Supreme Court had not decided in time, the Florida Senate would have appointed electors it felt were indicated by the popular vote.

John McKay, President of the Florida Senate, had been vindicated along with the House leadership. By a slow and deliberative process, with careful attentiveness to the concerns of the minority, the Florida legislature had been prepared to act, and had acted. The last gasp of hopes of overturning the election results were gone.

The third place of combat was in public opinion. In the battle of the metaphors, the Florida legislature had started way behind. The poll that indicated that only 5% of the people thought that the legislature should intervene made the political battlefield look hopeless. But we decided on a message. And we decided to stay on message.

It was a simple message. The Florida legislature was not hijacking the election. What it was doing was fulfilling the highest responsibility a state legislature has in America's constitutional system. The legislature and only the legislature had the power to select electors in a Presidential election. Its chief business was to ensure that the will of the people of its state got its appropriate role when the votes were counted for President in the electoral college.

It was not, therefore, a matter of the legislature asserting its power. It was the Florida legislature standing up to its responsibility. The buck stopped there.

There was nothing more important going on in the world than the election of an American President. There was nothing more important in the election of an American President than to determine who would get the most votes in the electoral college. There was no state more important in that determination than Florida because as Florida went, so went the nation. And there was no institution more important in the state of Florida than the Florida Legislature.

It had to put politics to one side. It could not consider what was popular. It had to do what it was elected to do, to make the tough decisions, to fulfill its constitutional responsibilities.

That was the message. The message was broken up into several parts, and articulate spokespersons for the Legislature hit their particular aspect of the message again and again and again on talk shows, in newspaper interviews, on television shows. And the message took.

It was a signal indication of success in the public relations arena. A poll taken shortly before the final Supreme Court decision in *Bush v. Gore* revealed that the populace of the United States had changed its mind. Now some 62% of the public believed that the Florida Legislature should intervene and appoint its own electors if the litigation surrounding the Presidential election had not been resolved prior to December 12, 2000. The results in this third arena were clear; the legislature had won again. It had been successful in vindicating its principles in the courts, its political objectives in the legislature, and in its public relations battle for the mind of the people.

One might think that the lessons here would not carry over easily into garden variety litigation. This was, after all, *sui generis*. The law was unique. The political circumstances were unique. The focus of the nation was unique. But in many ways, this somewhat novel battlefield reflects the importance of doing battle in any litigation.

There is first of all a lesson on the importance of conviction. One has to find a principle that is transcendent, believe it deeply and then convince others of its importance. Here it was a conviction that the Constitution had given to the legislature an important prerogative, and its power could not be limited even by other branches of state or federal government. It could not be modified by the highest court of the state. It could not be abrogated even by the state constitution. The conviction had been rooted in a Supreme Court decision and elaborated in briefs that were as persuasive as one could make them. One should never enter a courtroom without a conviction.

The second lesson is the importance of credibility. While politics is the art of the practical and possible, it is important not to be "political" in a bad sense. The care with which the President of the Florida Senate deliberated over whether or not to call a special session was important. The fairness in giving equal time to those experts who had opposite opinions was also important. The fairness in procedural rules, allowing everybody on both sides of the aisle to be heard, was important. The lack of political pugnacity spoke volumes. In order to weld together a majority on such a sensitive political question, it was important to be conscientious and to have credibility. One might argue about the ultimate outcome, but one could not argue that the process itself was not fair. So, too, a lawyer fighting hard for his client must maintain a sense of credibility, a sense that he fights fair, and the he is not demeaning to the other side or engaging in sharp practices.

A final lesson is one of creativity. There were thousands of issues in this election battle and tens of thousands of ways to express them. But variations on a simple theme, creatively expressed, was the difference in convincing the public. Coming at a problem from a different way and using the English language to cloak that message in a persuasive garb is something that can change the mind of a person who is seeking to evaluate what is occurring. By creatively smoothing a message into one that is palatable but yet fairly represents a fundamental conviction, one can change the tide of opinion and, occasionally, the tide of history.

Chapter 12

The Moral of the Story

"To some lawyers all facts are created equal."[12.1]

— Felix Frankfurter

The story is part of the lore of the Harvard Law School. It speaks to student insecurities. The genre ("if you think you have it bad, why when I was young. . .") is familiar enough to students who did not walk three miles to school every day or shovel coal into a furnace before doing their homework. And its intent is familiar also: to silence the whining of the current generation.

New students at the Harvard Law School have reason to whine. Sitting in a cavernous classroom like Langdell North Middle, they begin their fledgling legal career as the object of sport for a Socrates wannabe posing as a professor. The Socratic poseur comes into the classroom with a cardboard seating chart showing the names of his multiple victims and their locations in the room.

With the glee of a cat playing with a mouse, the professor picks a hapless new student and begins to grill him or her on the assigned cases, changing facts and assumptions and arguments, punching at the student from a variety of intellectual angles, teaching or browbeating, depending on whether one shares the perspective of the professor or the perspective of the student. For students used to the genteel environment of some cloistered college, this is a rude introduction to an increasingly rude profession.

Lest someone collapse into inordinate self-pity, however, someone will bring up the Bull Warren story. Bull Warren was a legendary Dean of the Harvard Law School in decades long past. His given name was, of course, not Bull. But Bull was a name fitted for his exquisite solicitousness for student sensitivities; he was an academic cousin of the infamous Bull Connor of Selma, Alabama.

As a fierce practitioner of the Socratic arts of interrogation, the Bull knew only one pedagogical method. To run at students, like one of the bulls of Pamplona, horns extended, seeking to use the mass of his disproportionate power and status, training and experience, to gore every student at least once before the term was over.

One of his students, a young man from Pennsylvania, could not take the Bull-like rushes. He burst into tears at his inability to answer or deflect the Dean's questions. The Bull stared at him in disbelief. Then he reached into his pocket, pulled out a dime, and flipped it to the student.

"What is that for?" the student asked.

Bull paused for dramatic effect. "That is for calling your Mommy to tell her you'll be coming home, because you're out of here."

After a few moments of silence, while Bull waited with arms folded across his chest, it appeared that the Dean was not kidding. The student gathered his books at the astonishment of his peers and trudged slowly, head down, up the stairs to the door that was to deliver him out of the law school and back to the outside world.

As he was halfway out the door, however, he paused. Then he turned around, his face red.

"Just wait a minute. I paid my tuition. Whom do you think you are, ordering me out of here, just like that, without any hearing, without any due process. I've got as much right to stay in this classroom as anybody else does!"

The class gasped. One did not talk like that to any dean, much less the dean who went by the name Bull. That was waving a red flag in the face of some very sharp and long horns.

But suddenly, Bull smiled. Then he spoke.

"Now you wait a minute. I think you might have the makings of a lawyer after all. Come back down here and resume your seat."

"And," he added, "give me back my dime."

Facts About Tort Liability and Its Impact on Consumers

➤ The cost of the U.S. tort system for 2001 was $205 billion, or $721 per citizen.

➤ U.S. tort costs increased 14.3 percent in 2001, the highest percentage increase since 1986.

➤ U.S. tort costs are 2.04% of Gross Domestic Product (GDP).

➤ The U.S. tort system is inefficient; it returns less than 50 cents on the dollar and less than 22 cents for actual economic loss to claimants.[12.2]

The story may be apocryphal. But it contains a moral useful to trial lawyers and their corporate clients. The moral can be summed up as follows.

No. 1
Whether Posing as Bulls or Barracudas, There are Bullies in the World.

Our system of justice is arguably as just as any system in the history of civilization. Looked at from the outside, evaluated by someone not a party to an existing lawsuit, the substantive and procedural rules look about as fair as human beings can make them.

But those mechanisms, designed to punish criminals through the criminal justice system, to reward civil claimants with small claims by providing the class action mechanism, to assure that customers get a fair bargain through consumer protection laws, to treat shareholders and investors fairly by provision of derivative and shareholder remedies, to provide a suitable environment for families and businesses, and to regulate hazardous activities by government regulation of business, however salutary, can also be used to bully, oppress and distort.

Incentives like large attorneys' fees, career enhancement for government lawyers, huge punitive damage recoveries, nationwide publicity of high-profile litigation, can become a fragrant incense that lures opportunists to attack legitimate businesses. For every gentle professor, there is an occasional Bull Connor. This is reality.

No. 2
When Faced with These Bullies, Many Victims Take the Easiest Way Out.

Our simpering student, full of self-pity, decided flight was preferable to fight, even if it cost him money he should not have to lose. Corporations sometimes follow the same pragmatic course. And quick and pragmatic resolutions frequently make sense, at least in the short run. If one can settle a strike suit which is totally unmeritorious out of insurance coverage, why not do so? If paying ransom to a litigious highwayman frees a hostage corporation, why not do so? And why should a company not treat baseless claims the same way it treats claims that may have at least some merit?

Business people are pragmatists, and need to be. But there is long-term and short-term pragmatism. One major medical center decided years ago to have a twofold strategy when sued for malpractice. If the claim was justified and had merit, they sought to settle quickly and fairly. They did not seek to "work" the plaintiffs to wear them down and prepare them for settlement. They tried to do the right thing. And do it quickly.

If the claim had no merit, they had a different strategy. Grind the plaintiffs to powder. Don't give them half a loaf. Don't give them a nuisance settlement. Don't rescue their lawyers by providing them out-of-pocket expenses. Assume the risk of the occasional eccentric verdict as a cost of doing business, in order to accomplish a greater objective: making people with unmeritorious claims think twice before suing. The strategy worked for them. They were sued far less than their more "pragmatic" competitors.

In the incestuous network of the plaintiffs' bar, people learn which entities they can bully and which entities they cannot bully and stay away from those they cannot unless they have a good case. Most bullies are, after all, cowards at the prospect of getting beaten up themselves.

No. 3
Bullies Keep Bullying
When They Have No Downside.

Bullies are intimidating when viewed from the outside. But deep within the reticular labyrinth of bully-psychology, there is a desire not to fight, to use taunts and threats so real brawls—and a real risk to life and limb—are avoided. Goliath was startled when little David rushed right at his 9' 4" body wielding nothing but a small sling. Better to engage in rhodomtade, to shout a stead stream of insults and watch enemy soldiers slink away and hide in caves.

The barracudas we have discussed continue to thrive because they have very little risk of personal injury to reputation or pocketbook from their lucrative assaults. The U.S. Attorney who brings a weak case can almost always intimidate a petrified executive into pleading to a misdemeanor even if he has to cross his fingers while admitting "guilt" at the sentencing hearing. The SEC can almost always bully a company or one of its officers to enter into a consent decree neither admitting nor denying guilt. The class action plaintiffs' lawyer can, even when his case is dead on arrival, almost always extort an insurance carrier into rescuing his firm by providing a multimillion dollar settlement. A state attorney general—or other state regulator—can almost always scare one of its regulated companies into "cease and desisting" even when the state's case is shaky.

The Paint-by-Numbers Lawsuit

The Internet has revolutionized the business of taking Corporate America to court

STEP ONE: FIND A VICTIM

Traditionally, lawyers waited for customers to come to them. But that's not always the way it works these days. Lots of plaintiffs' law firms advertise for clients on television or lure them through national referral networks such as USinjurylawyer.com.

STEP TWO: GET A LITIGATION PACKET

How-to guides exist for suits against handgun makers, tobacco companies, and Warner-Lambert diabetes drug Rezulin, among other things. Generally costing less than $200, they include almost everything a lawyer needs to get a case started.

STEP THREE: FIND AN EXPERT

A credible physician or engineer can do wonders with a jury. Web sites such as DepoConnect.com specialize in helping tort lawyers find good expert witnesses. Professional experts also rent booths at attorneys' conventions and advertise in legal trade journals.

STEP FOUR: GET MONEY

Courts move slowly. That means that lawyers and their clients sometimes have a cash-flow crisis while they wait for that big verdict to come in. Litigation-finance specialists such as ExpertFunding.com offer immediate cash in exchange for a stake in litigation, but the cash advance comes at a high price.

STEP FIVE: OBTAIN HOT DOCUMENTS

Nothing makes a case like a smoking gun. Organizations such as the Attorneys Information Exchange Group in Birmingham, AL, and ATLA Exchange serve as warehouses that help plaintiffs' attorneys get the internal corporate documents they need to win over a judge and jury. [12.3]

The aggravating aspect of these hedges against loss is that they occur with press releases that typically treat such resolutions as victories for the barracudas and defeats for his—innocent—antagonist.

No. 4.
Bet-the-Company/Career Cases Require Aggressive and Creative Responses.

Most clients, and most lawyers, like the security of painting by the numbers. They handle all cases much the same way: evaluate the complaint, organize a lawyer team with multiple associates below decks, answer the complaint asserting all possible defenses, serve tedious interrogatories, document requests and requests for admissions, take lengthy depositions, bring motions, fight a war of attrition, generate large attorneys' fees, and, last but not least, recommend payment of a large settlement to the other side, on the courthouse steps. This is Candide upside down: the worst of all possible worlds. Pay huge amounts to your lawyers and pay huge amounts to your adversaries.

This is litigation according to Tom Wolfe, a case of mau-mauing the flak-catchers.

Old dogs cannot adapt easily to new tricks. Big firm litigators, apprenticed in the art of catching flak, develop habitual techniques passed on by a litigator's oral tradition, that make their approach to big time litigation essentially robotic. They are predictable. They generate huge fees and large settlements, and, one might add, enormous rationalizations. When the Company has maximized its payment both to its own lawyers and to the adversary, the trial team and client resort to fatalism. O tempora, o mores. Given the craziness of contemporary litigation, this drubbing is the best we could do.

In a sampling of the cases described in the previous chapters, conventional litigation flak-catching litigation techniques would likely have resulted in devastating defeats: executives going to jail, companies being destroyed. The kind of conventional tactics useful for garden variety litigation are often not adequate in truly high stakes controversies. Clients should expect, and demand, something more: mobility and creativity from their counsel, an ability to turn on a dime and see a problem from a new perspective. And the courage to say to the Bull Warrens of the world: "Whom do you think you are?"

No. 5.
Play Offense.
Bite Back, If Possible.

There's an old story about two people swept away in a hot air balloon. Caught up in the clouds, they lose their bearings. When favorable winds allow them to get closer to earth they find themselves in unfamiliar territory. Finding a man walking along the sidewalk, one of the two leans over the side and yells, "Where are we?"

The answer from the man on the sidewalk comes back quickly. "You're in a hot air balloon."

A sudden upward draft sucks the balloon back up into the clouds.

"Can you imagine," one of the balloonsmen says, "Only one person to ask and it turns out to be a lawyer."

"Lawyer?," says the other. "How did you know it was a lawyer?"

"Because he answered our question, the answer was technically accurate, and the answer did not help us at all."

That explains, perhaps, why lawyers are normally terrible witnesses. They are more used to asking questions then answering them.

When someone is defending himself, he is almost always losing. The problem with much of what defense lawyers do in bet-the-company/bet-the-career litigation, is that the defense team thinks it is hired to defend. And defend it does. In doing so, it inevitably becomes defensive. A bad outcome is then assured. It is difficult to do better than tie when one never plays offense.

When trial lawyers are only defensive coordinators, they practice skills that are not without utility. But they don't win important victories in serious litigation. In each of the cases described in this book, it was the offensive maneuver that turned a potential loser into a clear winner.

Why not grill Bull Connor instead of having him grill you?

No. 6
Take the High Moral Ground.

One of the hidden persuaders in courtroom controversies is a perception that some of the combatants appear to have a guilty conscience. The person accused of wrongdoing, even utterly unjustifiably, sometimes internalizes the accusation and begins to believe it. The uneasiness mysteriously comes out in the voice, the manner, the approach.

The Germans say that Dobermans only bite children with bad consciences. Juries are like Dobermans in that regard. They often assess which side looks guilty, sometimes without even consciously doing so.

Skilled directors of theatrical productions know how to present a villain through hidden and nonverbal means, by such techniques as having his back to the audience, having him cover his face with a hand, or having him gesture in a way that is thought to communicate guilt. Unskilled directors of litigation productions often unwittingly present themselves or their clients as villains, without knowing they are doing so.

> At the beginning of the 1990's, just under half of civil rights cases were decided by juries. By the end of the decade, that number had climbed to three-quarters. [table/graph available.] [12.4]

Someone seeking to persuade a third party must understand his audience. Each member of a jury has a soul. The soul, we are told by classical philosophers, is composed of the mind, the will, and the emotions. A person seeking to capture the soul of a fact-finder needs to deal with all three.

It is important to win the mind. Winning the mind requires an advocate to convince the audience that he can win, that one can accept the position advanced by the defendant, and that it is intellectually responsible to do so. Presenting facts that support an argument are designed to win the mind: to convince a person of the truth, so he will in his "verdict" (Latin for truth-speaking) speak the truth.

But the mind is not the only motivator. Emotions are also involved. Whatever the facts may be, a member of the jury might feel the tug of affection for one side or another, may want to decide for a particular client or lawyer. They like one more than the other. They want their favorite to be happy with them when they come back from the jury room with a verdict.

Some counsel find it easy to go after the mind. They organize their outlines on yellow pads, marshal their mental appeals, and hammer home their favorable facts. Like a high school debater, they will defend their propositions with multiple responses to any argument of the other side, "five-pointing" this and "six-pointing" that. The lawyers project themselves as disembodied minds.

Other lawyers are emotional. They feel pain. They engage the affective side of the jury. They use sympathy and sentiment to do so. The intellectual lawyer finds such an approach undignified, sometimes maudlin. The emotional lawyer finds the intellectual lawyer dry and unpersuasive.

Both approaches can, of course, be effective. Sometimes jury emotions overcome an intellectual presentation of the facts; sometimes a presentation of overwhelming facts influence a jury to decide in a way they really do not want to decide. If one can engage both mind and emotions of a jury, if one can get a jury both to believe they can decide your way, and to want to decide your way, one can frequently win the case.

But there is another dimension to the human personality. It is the will. Judges and juries want to believe that they are doing the right thing. A famous legal realist achieved fame as an academic when he opined that judges use principles as pretexts to do what they want to do as a matter of personal whim. Their decisions have more to do with what they ate for breakfast, he was heard to say, than with any legal principles. This was "realism." But when the professor later was appointed to the federal circuit court, he was asked by a student if he decided cases the way he said judges typically decided cases during his lectures as a professor. "Oh, of course not," he said. "When I put on that black robe, I try to do justice."

Plaintiff Win Rates in Tort Cases Involving a Jury[12.5]

(State Courts)

Case Type	Plaintiff Win Rate
Toxic Substance	73%
Automobile	60%
Professional Malpractice	50%
Intentional	46%
Premises	43%
Slander/libel	41%
Product liability	40%
Medical malpractice	30%
All torts	49%

Jurors are not, at least self-consciously, legal realists. They want to do the right thing. It is a powerful motivator if one can convince a jury that it ought to decide your way. Juries frequently want to accomplish cosmic ends, not simply decide a trivial and tedious controversy.

The attempt to take the high moral ground is often wanting among corporations and their counsel. For one thing, such people are often uncomfortable with moralizing. Leave it for preachers and rabbis, I'm a trial lawyer. And because they do not appeal to the high moral ground, their arguments, however savvy and sophisticated, sometimes seem to lack conviction to the jury. Judges, eager to do the right thing, can take this perceived lack of moral conviction as an admission that the corporation is on the wrong side when it comes to the equities of the case.

The student in the Bull Warren story found his moral voice. He had paid his tuition. The arrogant professor had treated him badly; he had no right to do so. He convinced his adversary as well as his peers of the rightness of his position.

In the examples of serious litigation I have described, in every case there was an appeal to the high moral ground. Whether it is the case of the young CFO, Bill Olson, standing up to the SEC, or the famous investor, John Stein, refusing to roll over in the face of a strike suit; whether it is a famous medical clinic going to the mat with a sympathetic but overreaching plaintiff, or Big Bank asserting its moral claim to hold a borrower to his promises; whether it is Major League Baseball refusing to answer one question on a CID as a matter of principle, or an African-American small business owner staring down the government—right, or at least a claim to it, can make might.

Clarity is important to appeal to the mind. Creativity is important to win the affections of the jury. But conviction is perhaps the strongest appeal of all.

In many courtrooms across the United States there is a Latin motto etched in stone somewhere in the building. *Fiat justitia ruat coelum.* Do right though the stars fall. An advocate who can look a jury member in the eye and say that resonates with moral conviction.

The jury may conclude that the right thing is what that advocate says it is and that the right thing is not rewarding a sharp toothed barracuda.

Chapter One—*Barracuda Alert*

1.1   *See* National Center for State Courts, *Examining the Work of State Courts* 11 (Overview) (2003) <http://www.ncsonline.org/D_Research/csp/2003_Files/2003_Overview.pdf> (table, reporting 16.3 million state court civil cases filed in 2002, plus 57.6 million traffic, 15.4 million criminal, 4.6 million domestic, and 2.0 juvenile cases); *see also* <http://www.ncsonline.org/D_Research/csp/2003_Files/2003_Main_Page.html>. 3,153,600 seconds per year / 16.3 million civil cases = one new civil case every 1.9325 seconds. 3,153,600 seconds per year / 15.4 criminal cases = one new criminal case every 2.0454 seconds.

1.2   Frank J. Murray, *Special Report: The Rules of Lawyers—Jackpot justice gets best defense, Billions at stake with right case, generous jury*, The Washington Times, July 18, 2000 at A1.

1.3   Frank J. Murray, *Special Report: The Rules of Lawyers—Jackpot justice gets best defense, Billions at stake with right case, generous jury*, The Washington Times, July 18, 2000 at A1.

1.4   GRAPH: Jim Saxton, Vice-Chairman, Joint Economic Committee, *Improving the American Legal System: The Economic Benefits of Tort Reform*, Figure 4 (Distribution of Private Tort Costs), <http://www.house.gov/jec/tort/tort/fig-4.gif> (visited 9-28-00; link now dead); *see also* < http://www. house.gov/jec/tort/tort/tort.html>.

1.5   Frank J. Murray, *Special Report: The Rules of Lawyers—Jackpot justice gets best defense, Billions at stake with right case, generous jury*, The Washington Times, July 18, 2000 at A1.

1.5a   Overlawyered.com, *Cash Demanded for Drug Users and Panhandlers Inconvenienced by Film Crews*, Aug. 23-25, 2002 <http://overlawyered.com/archives/02/aug3.html>, citing Don Townson, *Canadian Hookers Campaign Against Hollywood*, variety/Yahoo, Aug. 21, 2002.

1.5b   Overlawyered.com, *Father Files Suit after Son Fails to Win MVP Award*, Nov. 8-10, 2002 <http://overlawyered.com/archives/02/nov1.html, citing *Father Sues Team for Not Naming Son MVP*, AP/ESPN, Nov. 7, 2002.

1.5c   Overlawyered.com, *Lawyers for Chimps?*, Apr. 29–30, 2002, <http://overlawyered.com/archives/02/apr3.html>, citing David Bank, *A Harvard Professor Lobbies to Save U.S. Chimps from Monkey Business*, Wall Street Journal, Apr. 25, 2002.

Chapter Two—*Your Attorney General Wants You*

2.1   Robert Reich, former Clinton Secretary of Labor, in USA Today, February 11, 1999.

2.2   Mark Twain, quoted in *Poetic Justice: The Funniest, Meanest Things Ever Said About Lawyers* 46 (Nolo Press 1988).

2.3   Trevor Armbrister, *Trial Lawyers On Trial,* Reader's Digest, January 2000 <http://www.readersdigest.com/rdmagazine/specfeat/archives/trial.htm>.

2.4   GRAPH: James R. Copland et al., *Trial Lawyers, Inc.: A Report on the Lawsuit Industry in America 2003—Attorneys' Fees* (Manhattan Institute, Center for Legal Policy) <http://www.triallawyersinc.com/p3d.gif>; *see also* <http://www.triallawyersinc.com/html/part03.html>.

2.5   John Fund & Martin Morse Wooster, *The Dangers of Regulation Through Litigation: The Alliance of Plaintiffs' Lawyers and State Governments 10* (American Tort Reform Foundation, 2000). Footnotes 3 and 4 (in original): Mark Curriden, *Fresh off Tobacco Success, State AGs Seek Next Battle,* Dallas Morning News, July 10, 1999, Online Edition.

2.6   John Fund & Martin Morse Wooster, *The Dangers of Regulation Through Litigation: The Alliance of Plaintiffs' Lawyers and State Governments 9,* n10 (American Tort Reform Foundation, 2000), citing Cong. Rec. S6149, U.S. Senate, June 11, 1998, *National Tobacco Policy and Youth Smoking Reduction Act.*

2.7   John Fund & Martin Morse Wooster, *The Dangers of Regulation Through Litigation: The Alliance of Plaintiffs' Lawyers and State Governments* n18 (American Tort Reform Foundation, 2000), citing Clay Robinson, *Notions of Exorbitant Fees Leave Lawyers in Tobacco Case Offends,* Houston Chronicle.

2.8   GRAPH: James R. Copland et al., *Trial Lawyers, Inc.: A Report on the Lawsuit Industry in America 2003—Introduction, A Recession-Resistant Industry* (Manhattan Institute, Center for Legal Policy), <http://www.triallawyersinc.com/p2a.gif>; *see also* <http://www.triallawyersinc.com/html/part02.html>.

2.9   Trevor Armbrister, *Trial Lawyers On Trial,* Reader's Digest, January 2000. <http://www.readersdigest.com/rdmagazine/specfeat/archives/trial.htm>.

2.10 John Fund & Martin Morse Wooster, *The Dangers of Regulation Through Litigation: The Alliance of Plaintiffs' Lawyers and State Governments 31* (American Tort Reform Foundation, 2000).

2.11 John Fund & Martin Morse Wooster, *The Dangers of Regulation Through Litigation: The Alliance of Plaintiffs' Lawyers and State Governments 32* (American Tort Reform Foundation, 2000).

2.12 John Fund & Martin Morse Wooster, *The Dangers of Regulation Through Litigation: The Alliance of Plaintiffs' Lawyers and State Governments 32–33* (American Tort Reform Foundation, 2000); *id.* at n71 (Joel Brinkley, *If Microsoft Loses Suit, 19 States Plan to Seek a Radical Overhaul,* New York Times, March 19, 1999.

2.13 Mike France, *The Litigation Machine,* Businessweek Online, January 29, 2001 <http://www.businessweek.com/2001/01_05/b3717001.htm>.

Chapter Three—*This Agency Has Sharp Teeth*

3.1   CSE Civil Justice Campaign, *Beware of Shark-Infested Waters!*, <http://www.cse.org/informed/801.html> (visited 9-25-00; link now dead).

3.2   GRAPH: Securities and Exchange Comm., *Investor Complaints and Questions* (fiscal 2003, modified 2/10/2004) <http://www.sec.gov/news/data.htm>; *see also* < http://www. sec.gov/news/studies.html>.

3.3   GRAPH: James R. Copland et al., *Trial Lawyers, Inc.: A Report on the Lawsuit Industry in America 2003—Mature Product Line: Class Actions* (Manhattan Institute, Center for Legal Policy), <http://www.triallawyersinc.com/p4b.gif>; *see also* <http://www.triallawyersinc.com/html/part04.html>.

3.4   Mike France, *The Litigation Machine,* Businessweek Online, January 29, 2001 <http://www.businessweek.com/2001/01_05/b3717001.htm>.

3.5   Overlawyered.com, November 26-28, 1999, <http://www.overlawyered.com/archives/99nov2.html>, citing Jesse Angelo, *Levitt: Web Brokers May Be on the Hook for Computer Crash*, New York Post, November 23, 1999.

3.6   Mike France, *The Litigation Machine,* Businessweek Online, January 29, 2001 <http://www.businessweek.com/2001/01_05/b3717001.htm>.

3.7   *See* Federalist Society, Analysis: *Class Action Litigation—A Federalist Society Survey,* 1 Class Action Watch 1, 5 (1999); Deborah Hensler et al., *Preliminary Results of the RAND Study of Class Action Litigation* at 15 (RAND Inst. for Civ. Just., 1997); James R. Copland et al., *Trial Lawyers, Inc.: A Report on the Lawsuit Industry in America 2003—Mature Product Line: Class Actions* at n55 (Manhattan Institute, Center for Legal Policy) <http://www.triallawyersinc.com/p4b.gif>; *see also* <http://www.triallawyersinc.com/html/part04.html>.

3.8   Overlawyered.com, September 4, 2000 <http://www.overlawyered.com/archives/00sept1.html#000904a>, citing Craig Bicknell, "Emulex Victims: Who Can We Sue?," *Wired News,* September 1, 2000.

Chapter Four—*Barracudas You Used to Know (And Swim With)*

4.1   RAND, September 25, 2002 press release: *RAND Study Shows Asbestos Claims Rise Dramatically; Cost of Claims Filed by 600,000 People Now Tops $54 Billion* <http://www.rand.org/hot/press.02/asbestos.html>.

4.2   RAND Institute for Civil Justice Analysis of Civil Jury Trends, 1996 <http://www.rand.org/publications/RB/RB9025/RB9025.html#fn0>, <http://www.rand.org/centers/icj/faqs/ans5.htm>.

4.3   JV Schwan, J.D, *Capitol Comment 231—Don't Let the Government Mimic Trial-Lawyer Greed,* May 28, 1999 (Citizens for a Sound Economy) <http://www.cse.org/informed/201.html>. Footnotes: [1]Senate Committee on the Judiciary, 106th Cong., 1st Sess. (1998) (statement of Professor George Priest). [2]Moller, Pace, and Carroll, *Punitive Damages in Financial Injury Jury,* RAND Corp. MR-888-ICJ (1997).

4.4   *Jones v. Ahmanson,* 460 P.2d 464 (Cal. 1969).

4.5   GRAPH: James R. Copland et al., *Trial Lawyers, Inc.: A Report on the Law-suit Industry in America 2003—Introduction* (Manhattan Institute, Center for

Legal Policy) <http://www.triallawyers.cin/p2c.gif>, <http://www.triallawyers.com/html/part02.html>.

4.6   GRAPH: James R. Copland et al., *Trial Lawyers, Inc.: A Report on the Lawsuit Industry in America 2003—Introduction* (Manhattan Institute, Center for Legal Policy), <http://www.triallawyersinc.com/p1c.gif>, <http://www.triallawyersinc.com/html/part01.html>.

4.7   Steve Alexander, *Former Helix officers end up paying*, Star Tribune (Minneapolis, MN), November 9, 1993, at 3D.

Chapter 5 – The Right Role in the Melodrama

5.1   *See* Trevor Armbrister, *Suing Like Crazy*, Reader's Digest, October 2000, at 153–54.

5.2   *See* Overlawyered.com, August 31, 2000, <http://www.overlawyered.com/archives/00aug3.html>, citing *AP/Philadelphia Daily News*, August 25, 2000.

5.3   Spencer Abraham, *Litigation Tariff: The Federal Case for National Tort Reform* (Policy Review, Summer 1995, Number 73), <http://www.policyreview.com/summer95/thabra.html>. *See also* Deborah J. La Fetra, *Defending Florida's Tort Reform Law*, Pacific Legal Foundation Atlantic Center Dispatch Newsletter, Fall 1999.

5.4   Mike France, *The Litigation Machine*, Businessweek Online, January 29, 2001 <http://www.businessweek.com/2001/01_05/b3717001.htm>.

5.5   Highlights, Marika F.X. Litras, Ph.D. and Carol J. DeFrances, Ph.D., *Federal Tort Trials and Verdicts, 1996–97*, Federal Justice Statistics Program, February 1999, NCJ 17285 (rev. 5/3/99) (U.S. Department of Justice, Office of Justice Programs, Bureau of Justice Statistics) <http://www.ojp.usdoj.gov/pub/ascii/fttv97.txt>.

5.6   *Michigan Lawsuit Abuse Watch* <http://www.mlaw.org.loonylawsuits.htm> (visited 9-11-00; link now dead).

5.7   Deborah J. La Fetra, *Defending Florida's Tort Reform Law*, Pacific Legal Foundation, Atlantic Center Dispatch Newsletter, Fall 1999, <http://www.pacificlegal.org/ac-tort.htm>.

5.7a   *See* Office of the Assistant Secretary for Planning & Evaluation, U.S. Dept. of Health & Human Services, *Confronting the New Health Care Crisis: Improving Health Care Quality And Lowering Costs by Fixing Our Medical Liability System* (July 24, 2002) at 14; St. Paul Ins. Co. December 12, 2001 press release, *The St. Paul Announces Fourth-Quarter Actions to Improve Profitability and Business Positioning* <http://www2.stpaul.com/spc/corp/spcnews.nsf>; *see also* James R. Copland et al., *Trial Lawyers, Inc.: A Report on the Lawsuit Industry in America 2003 – Mature Product Line: Medical Malpractice* (Manhattan Institute, Center for Legal Policy), <http://www.triallawyersinc.com/html/part06.html>.

5.8   Study by New York-based Aronoff Associates for HIMA, *Biomaterials Availability: a Vital Health Care Industry Hangs in the Balance*, cited in *Michigan Lawsuit Abuse Watch*, <http://www.mlaw.org/didyouknow.htm> (link now dead; visited 9-11-00).

5.9   Center For Health Policy Research, *American Medical Association Socioeconomic Monitoring System*, April 1995, cited by American Tort Reform Association, *A Few Facts About The Effects of Malpractice Suits*.

5.10   *Overlawyered.com*, 7/16/99, <http://www.overlawyered.com/archives/99july2.html>, citing Patrick E. Tyler, *Tobacco-Busting Lawyers On New Gold-Dusted Trails*, New York Times, March 10, 1999.

5.11   Former United States Attorney General Richard Thornburgh, *America's Civil Justice Dilemma: The Prospects For Reform*, in *Maryland Law Review* 1996, Number 4, cited by Michigan Lawsuit Abuse Watch, <http://www.mlaw.org/didyouknow.htm> (visited 9-11-00).

5.12   GRAPH: National Center for State Courts, *Examining the Work of the State Courts—Percent of Jury Awards Over $1 Million (State Courts)* Vol. 1, No. 1 <http://www.ncsc.dni.us/research/csp/csphigh2.htm>; *see also* <http://www.ncsc.dni.us/RESEARCH/csp/tortperc.htm> (visited 9-28-00).

Chapter Six—*The Department of Defense Plays Offense*

6.1   GRAPH: James R. Copland et al., Trial Lawyers, Inc.: A Report on the Lawsuit Industry in America 2003—Introduction (Manhattan Institute, Center for Legal Policy) <http://www.triallawyersinc.com/p1c.gif>, <http://www.triallawyersinc.com/html/part01.html>.

Chapter Seven—*Not a Class Act*

7.1   GRAPH: "Mass Tort Litigation 'Exploded' in the 1980s," RAND Institute for Civil Justice, *Understanding Mass Personal Injury Litigation* (1995–1996 analyses of mass personal injury litigation), <http://www.rand.org/publications/RB/RB9021/RB9021.word1.gif>, <http://www.rand.org/publications/RB/RB9021/RB9021.word.html>.

7.2   U.S. Census Bureau, January 15, 2003 press release: *Computer Services Revenues Total $184 Billion in 2001; Legal, Management, Engineering and Accounting Services Show Increases* <http://www.census.gov/Press-Release/www/releases/archives/service_industries/000350.html>; *see also* Frank J. Murray; Special Report: The Rule of Lawyers, *Big salaries not just for partners, associates share wealth, but pay for judges lags*, The Washington Times, July 19, 2000 at A1.

7.3   GRAPH: *Annual flow of law degrees outpaces medical degrees in 1970s—The Lawyer Spigot*; *see* Peter Brimelow, *Lawyers Everywhere*, Forbes.com <http://www.forbes.com/forbes/99/0920/6407150a.htm> (visited 9-28-00).

7.4   Steven Malanga, *Class Action? Third Aisle to the Left*, The Wall Street Journal, July 8, 2004 <http://www.opinionjournal.com/extra/?id=110005311>.

7.5   Overlawyered.com, November 30, 1999 <http://www.overlawyered.com/archives/99nov2.html>, citing *The Bunker*, Golf Digest, October 1, 1999.

7.6   Trevor Armbrister, *Suing Like Crazy*, Reader's Digest, October 2000 (adapted from pp.154–55).

7.7   *Anchem Producs v. Windsor*, 117 S.Ct 2231 (1997).

7.8   GRAPH: RAND Institute for Civil Justice, *Class Action Dilemmas: Pursuing Public Goals for Private Gain*, executive summary p. 7 (Class Actions) <http://www.rand.org.publications/MR/MR969.1.pdf> (pdf file: p. 16).

7.9   New York Post, September 6, 2000 <http://www.nypost.com/delonas/sept00/090900/090600.htm>.

7.10a   John Calfee, *Solving the asbestos litigation morass*, The Washington Times, November 25, 1996, at A17.

7.10b   Associated Press, Judge Approves Plan to Settle Claims Against Dow Corning, The New York Times, December 1, 1999, at A19.

7.10c   Trevor Armbrister, *Trial Lawyers On Trial*, Reader's Digest, January 2000, <http://www.readersdigest.com/rdmagazine/specfeat/archives/trial.htm>.

7.10d   *Shaw v. Toshiba Am. Info. Sys.*, 2000 U.S. Dist. LEXIS 3592.

Chapter Eight—*I Don't Like You Anymore*

8.1   U.S. Department of Justice, Office of Justice Programs, *Civil Rights Complaints in U.S. District Courts, 1990–98*, Bureau of Justice Statistics, Special Report, January 2000, NCJ 17342 (rev. 2/22/00) <http://www.ojp.usdoj.gov/bjs/pub/ascii/crcusdc.txt>.

8.1a   *See Tamara Loomis, In Spite of Reform Law, Milberg Weiss Emerges as Winner in Securities Suits*, 229 N.Y.L.J., Apr. 22, 2003, at 1 <http://www.iii.org.media/facts/statsbyissue/litigiousness>; *see also* James R. Copland et al., *Trial Lawyers, Inc.: A Report on the Lawsuit Industry in America 2003—Mature Product Line: Class Actions* (Manhattan Institute, Center for Legal Policy) at n66, <http://www.triallawyersinc.com/html/part04.html>.

8.2   Overlawyered.com, September 5, 2000 <http://www.overlawyered.com>, citing Curt Suplee, *EEOC Backs 'Cold Fusion' Devotee*, Washington Post, August 23, 2000.

8.3   [1]Timothy P. Cartney, *Why Trial Lawyers Love Liberals*, Human Events, June 16, 2000, at p. 5; [2]American Tort Reform Association, <http://www.atra.org.show/7343> (2002, "Issues"); *see also* <http://www.atra.org/display/19>; [3]William B. Griffin, *Tort Reform in The U.S. Liability System* (Medical Device CEO Summit, July 18, 1995) <http://www.brobeck.com/docs/meddevic.htm> (visited 8-30-00).

8.4   Overlawyered.com, November 17, 1999 <http://www.overlawyered.com/archives/99nov2.html#991122a>, citing *EEOC Settles "English Only" Workplace Suit for $55,000*, DowJones.com newswire, November 12, 1999, and Darryl Van Duch, *English-Only Rules Land In Court*, National Law Journal, October 26, 1999.

8.5   Walter Olson, *Disabling America*, National Review, May 5, 1997, <http://walterolson.com/articles/nrdisable.html>, citing Washington Post, April 8, 1997, at A1.

8.6   Stephen J. Carroll et al., *Asbestos Litigation Costs and Compensation: An Interim Report, viii* (RAND Inst. for Civ. Just., 2002) <http://www.rand.org/publications/DB/DB397/DB397.pdf>; Lisa Girion, *Firms Hit Hard as Asbestos Claims Rise*, Los Angeles Times, Dec. 17, 2001, at A1; Carvill Am., *How to Minimize Casualties* <http://www.carvill.com/news_casualties.htm>; Insurance

Information Institute, *Asbestos Liability* (Aug. 2003) <http://www.iii.org/media/hottopics/insurance/asbestos>; *see also* James R. Copland et al., *Trial Lawyers, Inc.: A Report on the Lawsuit Industry in America 2003—Mature Product Line: Asbestos* (Manhattan Institute, Center for Legal Policy) <http://www.triallawyersinc.com/html/part05.html>.

Chapter Nine—*Caveat Vendor*

9.1   Michael DeBow, law professor at Samford University (Birmingham), quoted by Trevor Armbrister, *Suing Like Crazy*, Reader's Digest, October 2000, at 154.

9.2   http://www.nolo.com/humor/jokes/45jokes.html (visited 9-18-00).

9.3   *Coffee Spill Burns Woman: Jury Awards $2.9 million*, The Wall Street Journal, August 19, 1994 at B3.

9.4   GRAPH: "Big Tobacco Economics 1997 (Phillip Morris stock)," *PBS Frontline*, <http://www.pbs.org/wgbh/pages/frontline/shows/settlement/big/bankrupt.html> (visited 9-19-00).

9.5   GRAPH: James R. Copland et al., *Trial Lawyers, Inc.: A Report on the Lawsuit Industry in America 2003—Mature Product Line: Asbestos* (Manhattan Institute, Center for Legal Policy), <http://www.triallawyersinc.com/p5a.gif>, <http://www.triallawyersinc.com/html/part05.html>.

9.6   Frank J. Murray, *Special Report: The Rules of Lawyers, Jackpot justice gets best defense, Billions at stake with right case, generous jury*, The Washington Times, July 18, 2000, at A1.

9.7   Peter Huber, *Fleeing Alabama*, Forbes, July 15, 1996, at 92, quoted by Overlawyered.com, <http://www.overlawyered.com/articles/huber/alabama.html> (visited 10-4-2004).

9.8   Trevor Armbrister, *Suing Like Crazy*, Reader's Digest, October 2000 at 158 (excerpt).

9.9   Overlawyered.com, November 17, 1999, <http://www.overlawyered.com/archives/00july2.html#000717a>, citing Rick Anderson, *Tobacco money flows both ways*, Mother Jones, July 6, 2000.

9.10   American Tort Reform Association, *A Civil Injustice? Anderson v. General Motors* (December, 2000) <http://www.atra.org/anderson>.

9.11   Frank J. Murray, *Special Report: The Rules of Lawyers, Jackpot justice gets best defense, Billions at stake with right case, generous jury*, The Washington Times, July 18, 2000 at A1.

9.12   Frank J. Murray, *Special Report: The Rules of Lawyers, Jackpot justice gets best defense, Billions at stake with right case, generous jury*, The Washington Times, July 18, 2000 at A1.

9.13   Overlawyered.com, August 25-27, 2000 <http://www.overlawyered.com/archives/00aug3.html>, citing May 18, 1999 press release from New York City Office of Comptroller, Alan Hevesi, 5/18/99.

9.14   Overlawyered.com, November 18, 2000, <http://www.overlawyered.com/archives/00july2.html#000717b>, citing Sonia Giordani, *California Latex Glove Verdict Sets Tone*, The San Francisco Recorder, July 17, 2000.

9.15   Mark Parisi, *Offthemark.com,* <http://www.offthemark.com/law2.htm> (visited 9-8-00).

9.16   GRAPH: From "Domestic v. Foreign Legal Costs (U.S. Corporations)," 1994 Business Roundtable survey of 20 major U.S. corporations, quoted in Spencer Abraham, *Litigation Tariff: The Federal Case for National Tort Reform, Policy Review,* Summer 1995, No. 73, <http://www.policyreview.com/summer95/thabra.html>.

17.17   Overlawyered.com, July 2000 <http://www.overlawyered.com/archives/00july1.html#000710a>.

Chapter Ten—*When it's Hot, it's Hot*

10.1   David E. Bernstein, *The Cato Review of Business & Government, Procedural Tort Reform, Lessons from Other Nations,* Regulation, 1996 Vol. 19, No. 1 <http://www.cato.org/pubs/regulation/reg19n1e.html>.

10.2   RAND, *Releasing Small Firms from Superfund Liability* (Research Brief RB-9032) (2000) <http://www.rand.org/publications/RB/RB9032/#fn0>.

10.3   Overlawyered.com, August 2, 2000, <http://www.overlawyered.com/archives/00aug1.html>, citing David Armstrong, *US Judge Rules EPA Harassed Mill Owner,* Boston Globe, August 1, 2000.

10.4   W.S. Gilbert, *Iolanthe* (Lord Chancellor's Song).

10.5   Overlawyered.com, November 30, 1999 <http://www.overlawyered.com/archives/99nov2.html>, citing EPA Region 2 Press Release, November 10, 1999.

10.6   Robert Reich, former Clinton Secretary of Labor, in USA Today, February 11, 1999.

10.7   Ben Lieberman, *Environmental Sweetheart Suits* (October 21, 1999) (Competitive Enterprise Institute) <http://www.cei.org/UpdateReader.asp?ID=823>.

10.8   Mike France, *The Litigation Machine,* Businessweek Online, January 29, 2001 <http://www.businessweek.com/2001/01_05/b3717001.htm>, inset: *Tort Lawyers' Secret Weapon,* <http://www.businessweek.com/2001/01_05/b3717004.htm>.

Chapter Eleven—*Florida 2000*

11.1   *Supreme Court of the United States—Cases on Docket, Disposed of, and Remaining on Docket at Conclusion of October Terms, 1998 Through 2002,* Table A-1, <http://www.uscourts.gov/judbus2003/appendices/a1.pdf>.

11.2   GRAPH: James R. Copland et al., *Trial Lawyers, Inc.: A Report on the Lawsuit Industry in America 2003—Government Relations/Public Relations* (Manhattan Institute, Center for Legal Policy), <http://www.triallawyersinc.com/p10b.gif>, <http://www.triallawyers.com/html/part10.html>.

11.3   Supreme Court of the United States, *The Court and its Traditions* <http://www.supremecourtus.gov/about/traditions/pdf> (visited 7-1-2004).

11.4   Supreme Court of the United States, The Justices' Caseload <http://www.supremecourtus.gov/about/justicecaseload.pdf> (visited 7-1-2004).

11.5   Supreme Court of the United States, Biographies of Current Members of the Supreme Court <http://www.supremecourtus.gov/about/biographiescurrent. pdf> (visited 7-1-2004); *Members of the Supreme Court (1789 to Present)*, <http://www.supremecourtus.gov/about/members.pdf> (visited 10-27-2004).

Chapter Twelve—*The Moral of the Story*

12.1   Felix Frankfurter, quoted in *Poetic Justice: The Funniest, Meanest Things Ever Said About Lawyers* 78 (Nolo Press 1988).

12.2   Tillinghast-Towers Perrin, *U.S. Tort Costs: 2002 Update*, (New York, 2002); *Facts About Tort Liability And Its Impact On Consumers* (American Tort Reform Association) <http://www.atra.org/files.cgi/7366_Facts-Impact-On-Economy03.htm> (visited 11-18-2003).

12.3   Mike France, *The Litigation Machine*, Businessweek Online, January 29, 2001, <http://www.businessweek.com/2001/01_05/b3717003.htm>; *see also* <http://www.businessweek.com/2001/01_05/b3717001.htm>.

12.4   U.S. Department of Justice, Office of Justice Programs, *Civil Rights Complaints in U.S. District Courts, 1990–98*, Bureau of Justice Statistics, Special Report, January 2000, NCJ 17342 (rev. 2/22/00) <http://www.ojp.usdog.gov/bjs/pub/ascii/crcusdc.txt>.

12.5   Ostrom & N. Kauder, *Examining the Work of State Courts, 1998: A National Perspective from the Court Statistics Project* (National Center for State Courts, 1999). <http://www.ncsc.dni.us/divisions/research/csp/csp-exam.html>.

John Coleman →
sue Al Gore selling
a fraudulent product
carbon credits

UK Hadley Climate
researchers

2008 Climate Change
James Taylor – Heartland
Institute